VICTORY FO.

Twesigye Jackson Kaguri was raised in Uganda, graduated from Makerere University, and now lives in East Lansing, Michigan with his wife and four children. He has received two honorary Doctorate degrees, was a 2012 CNN Hero, and won the 2015 Waislitz Global Citizen Award. He currently works as the full-time director of the Nyaka Project (www.nyakaschool.org).

Susan Urbanek Linville is a freelance writer in New Castle, Pennsylvania. She has co-authored three books, writes a weekly spiritualism blog, and has published numerous newspaper and science articles.(www.susanurbaneklinville.com).

Praise for *Victory for My Village*

I thought that your first book, *A School for My Village* was a lot like reaching the top of Mount Kilimanjaro... with *Victory for my Village*, I feel like you have now reached the top of Mount Everest. Congratulations on this monumental achievement!

—Lucy Y. Steinitz, Senior Technical Advisor for Protection at Catholic Relief Services

Victory for My Village is pure inspiration and shows the incredible power of faith with a lot of hard work. This book should be a must read for every student interested in international development, and in the carry-on bag of religious folks traveling on a mission trip.

— Paul Sutherland, Chairman of the Utopia Foundation.

Sometimes, I had to stop reading and go find a family member to tell them what I had just read. Powerful. Poignant. Touching. Caring — and shot through with love.

— Sherrye Henry, author of *The Deep Divide*

VICTORY

FOR MY

VILLAGE

FULFILLING THE PROMISE

Twesigye Jackson Kaguri

with

Susan Urbanek Linville

Pokeberry Press, New Castle, Pennsylvania

Victory for My Village

Cover Photograph courtesy of Makanga Andrew

Other photographs courtesy of Matt Stauble, Brittany Linville Tonet, and The Nyaka Program

Map designed by Susan Urbanek Linville

Published by Pokeberry Press, a division of Pokeberry Exchange, LLC., New Castle, Pennsylvania

www.pokeberrypress.com

Pokeberry books may be purchased for book club, educational, business, and promotional use. For information, email editor@pokeberryexchange.com with your request.

ISBN 978-0-9972276-9-7

Printed in the United States of America.

Book Design by Stephen V. Ramey

To all the people who have helped the Nyaka Program, giving time, energy, skills, and financial support large and small. Because of you, we are all part of this incredible victory.

But thanks be to God, who gives us victory through our Lord Jesus Christ.

First Corinthians 15:57

Contents

VICTORY

FOR MY

VILLAGE

AFRICA

SOUTH SUDAN

DEM.
REP. OF
THE
CONGO

UGANDA

Kanungu
District

KAMPALA

Rukungiri
District

Kambuga

Lake
Victoria

K
E
N
Y
A

RWANDA

TANZANIA

INTRODUCTION

You might say I am a man of two countries. I grew up in the hill country of western Uganda in the small subsistence farming village of Nyakagyezi. We had no electricity or running water, no computer and, yes, no Wi-Fi. I shared a pencil with my siblings in primary school and did not own a pair of shoes until I started university. In those early years, life was harsh and my father abusive, but I received the one thing that freed me from poverty—an education. That eventually brought me to the United States, first on a fellowship to Columbia University, and then, to pursue a career.

Although I became a citizen of the United States, I promised never to forget my village. In the late 1990s, when HIV/AIDS devastated Uganda, that promise was tested. The virus took my older brother, Frank, my sister, Mbabazi, and my young nephew, Gaddafi. It also took the parents of nearly two million children. There is no Ugandan family that did not lose someone to this scourge.

Traditionally in Uganda, an uncle or an aunt takes on the responsibility of caring for an orphaned child, but HIV/AIDS was destroying an entire generation. In too many cases there were no aunts and uncles left. Orphans were forced to live with grandparents, at a time when grandparents should have been the ones receiving help. There is no Social Security in Uganda.

With no working adults in the home, these orphans lived in grinding poverty. They were lucky to get food to eat. Schooling, which required fees for tuition, uniforms and books, was out of the question.

While the orphan situation in Uganda grew worse, I married and moved to Bloomington, Indiana with my ex-wife, Beronda. We were busy with our lives, looking forward to successful careers and saving to buy a house. Still, I could not shake the sour feeling in my stomach. Each time I talked to people back home, I received word of another death. My village was suffering, especially the children. Something had to be done.

Beronda did not understand the urgency of the situation until we visited my parents. Things changed quickly when she saw firsthand what was happening in the village. Together, we decided that the best way to help the orphans of Nyakagyezi was to open a school. We created a foundation, used our small savings to build the first two rooms of Nyaka Aids Orphans School, enlisted volunteer teachers and host families, and enrolled our first fifty-six students.

My son, Nicolas, was born soon after and Beronda accepted a position at Michigan State University. We moved to the East Lansing area. With that move came a house mortgage, car payments, utilities, and all the usual expenses.

I am an idealist, but even an idealist must pay his bills. One salary was not enough to cover our costs while I worked to promote Nyaka School. I found a position at the university too, eventually becoming Director of Development in the College of Agriculture and Natural Resources. My main job was to raise money for student scholarships, research, and study abroad.

By 2006, we had settled into a routine. I worked at MSU during the day and stopped at the post office to pick up Nyaka mail on my way home. After dinner, I retired to my basement office to sort through letters and donations. I wired money to the school on my lunch hour and traveled many weekends to fundraising events.

That time was certainly a test of my determination. I was trying to do it all: husband, father, soccer coach, non-profit fundraiser, and full-time department director. Each has its own reward, but even I had periods of doubt. Could I keep up this pace indefinitely? I had to constantly remind myself that it was worth the effort.

In three short years, Nyaka grew from a two-room school with volunteer teachers, to a foundation with a committed board, growing programs, and many success stories. We established Friends of Nyaka groups in New York, Aspen, Indiana, and California. Several volunteers stepped forward in East Lansing to help the young organization maintain an office.

I prayed to God every day for the strength to continue, and though strained by the pace, attending Seventh Day Adventist Church services on Saturdays remained a source of inspiration and renewal for my family. And, as I soon discovered, God had even more challenges waiting for me. This is the story of my challenges as well as the accomplishments of Nyaka's Pioneers, the first class of students to graduate from Nyaka Primary School.

CHAPTER 1

A LESSON IN DETERMINATION

There is an eight-hour time difference between Michigan and Nyakagyezi. Even though the village has no electricity, Nyaka staff communicate with cell phones they recharge from the solar panels at the school. I routinely call them to check on things at either midnight or in the early morning, Michigan time.

On this fall morning, it was my turn to get Nicolas ready for school. Beronda had left for work at Michigan State University where she juggled teaching and research. My hours were more flexible, but no less demanding. Our jobs were at the same university, but we rarely spent quality time together.

After a long pause, the call went through.

"*Agandi*," I said into the phone as I handed Nic his coat.

"*Nigye*," Teacher Lydia greeted me. We discussed the general details of running the Nyaka programs before she brought up one last item.

"We have a problem with a student."

My heart sank. As hard as we worked to help each student, a small few got into trouble. Some skipped school. Some ran off to the city with dreams of making money.

"What happened? Which student?"

"It is not one of ours," Lydia said. "A boy named Hilary."

"I do not understand. Has this boy made trouble at the school?" It was not uncommon for neighboring children to bully Nyaka students because their parents have died of HIV/AIDS.

"He wants to be a student here."

"Tell him to come back during registration time." Lydia should know that.

"He is from Bikongozo. He walked here."

It took a moment for her words to register. "Bikongozo in Nyakishenyi?"

"Yes," she said. "He is eleven years old. He said it took him two days and three nights."

"How is this possible? Bikongozo is in Rukungiri District." That is south and east of Nyaykagyezi, a good thirty miles as the crow flies, but there is no straight path through the hilly terrain. "Do you think he is telling the truth?"

Lydia paused. "Well, he was very tired and dirty. And very hungry."

Nic sat on the floor near the front door to put on his shoes. I glanced at a photo on the dining room wall of Taata, Maama, and my sisters. When I was a boy, I sneaked away to follow my sisters to school. That was a stone's throw compared to the distance this child had walked.

I imagined him hiking barefoot along the rock-studded dirt paths that wind through our steep mountains, the road that clings to the edge of hillsides as it passes Murama, the wider track skirting Bwindi Impenetrable National Park. Wild boars and dogs might easily have attacked him in less populated areas. There were muddy streams to cross, malaria-ridden mosquitos, snakes. The coffee plant in Rugyeyo offered up the dangers of encountering nefarious people ready to take advantage of a boy. It made my skin itch to think of these things.

"He heard about the Nyaka School program on the radio," Lydia said. "He wants to get a free education."

"When did he arrive?"

"This morning. We gave him breakfast. Now we do not know what to do with him."

Nic tugged at my coat. "Dad, I'm ready to go."

I leaned down, palm covering the phone. "Just a minute. I am talking to Teacher Lydia."

When we first opened Nyaka School we were inundated with applications. For every student accepted, we turned many away. It was no easier now to witness those disappointed faces, but we had steeled ourselves to the fact that we could not take everyone. If Hilary were a local boy, we would have turned him down and it would not have been a topic of my morning phone call.

"Is he an AIDS orphan?"

"Yes. He lives with his grandparents."

I sighed. It would be reasonable to send this boy home in the school van, but I admired his fortitude. I was a stubborn child to be sure, but I never would have made it so far through the wilderness alone. Sleeping in someone's banana plantation, or in a field with the goats. How could a boy of 11 manage it? How did he find his way to Nyakagyezi? He must have summoned the courage to ask strangers for directions, a feat even more daunting in some ways than the journey.

"Put him in a classroom," I said. "Tell Taata and Maama the boy will spend the night with them. I will call them later." Taata would be happy to have another hand to help take care of his cows, but it would be only a temporary arrangement. Our goal was to keep kids with their families. If this boy had grandparents, he should live with them.

I dropped Nic off at his pre-school and spent the day at work, but my mind wandered repeatedly to the rugged slopes of Kanungu District. When I first planned Nyaka, I wanted it to be a comprehensive program. I imagined gardens to feed the students, a nurse to provide health services, local sponsors to provide homes for orphans who had no family. I still dreamed of expanding the Nyaka Program, a farm, a clinic, a library, maybe even a secondary school. But those were dreams. Next year, Nyaka School would graduate its first class. We had managed to obtain enough funding to feed our students, pay our teachers, and finish the final classrooms, but there was nothing left to take in additional students. If we accepted Hilary, what would we tell the local students waiting in line? It was not fair to them to enroll a child from outside the district, no matter how far he walked. Sending Hilary home was the logical action.

My heart did not want to listen. I wanted to help him. We did not have the resources to build a farm or a library, but maybe we could manage another primary school in Nyakishenyi. We could construct a couple of rooms at a time as we did for Nyaka.

That evening at dinner, one of the few times our family was together, I mentioned the idea of a new school to Beronda. She reminded me that we already required two jobs to pay our own bills.

Dr. Jude Mugerwa, a friend and one of our board members, did not like the idea either. "Nyaka is not stable yet," he said over the phone. "How can you build another school?"

They were probably right, but as I watched the smiling faces of

Nyaka kids form and fade on my desktop screen, I could not help but feel the aching need of all Ugandan orphans. Other photos appeared. Freda Byaburakiirya, who volunteered to teach our first class. Me digging the ditch for the foundation of a new classroom. Students in bright purple uniforms sitting at their new desks. My throat squeezed tight. I smiled and wiped my eye.

There must be a way. I had learned a lot about fundraising in my position at MSU. There were generous donors out there. Sometimes you had to work to find them. Sometimes they were right under your nose.

The slideshow returned to its beginning, a photo of Nyaka's first two rooms. It reminded me of conversations I had had with the Reverend David Bremer, one of our first supporters in Indiana. He taught me the value of connections and introduced me to the Bloomington Rotarians. Nyaka School had succeeded because we took the risk to build it before we had funding. In the process, we formed lasting relationships with people who would help keep the project running in numerous ways.

Hilary was from the Nyakishenyi area, home not only to my father's family, but to Professor Mondo Kagonyera. Professor Mondo, chancellor of Makerere University and a Parliamentarian for Rubabo, was related to me on my mother's side. He had been instrumental in opening Nyaka School in 2003 and continued to be a major supporter of our projects. I trusted his opinion and decided to call him.

"I think another school is a wonderful idea," he said. "The people of that area are extremely poor. They can use our help."

"Mugerwa does not think we should risk it," I said. "He fears we will overextend ourselves. A new school will be expensive."

"We will find others," Professor Mondo said. "If the local

people know you are building a school for them, I am sure they will donate time and materials. I know people in Kampala who will want to contribute. Look what you have done with Nyaka School. It was only two rooms when you started."

"You are right." I felt more confident.

I began planning. I knew of a plot of land that we might buy. We would construct a temporary building and enroll sixty students as soon as possible. Hilary would get his free school, and I would have time to raise money to build additional rooms. The Nyaka model had worked once. Why not a second time?

Before going to sleep that night, I prayed for success. Building two rooms and finding orphans to attend the school would be easy. Once we filled the classrooms, however, we were committed to the kids. No turning back.

Construction figures ran through my head. Stones, wood, cement, metal roofing material. The costs of labor and transportation. Once the school was open, we needed breakfasts, school supplies, teachers' salaries. I had no idea where the funding would come from but was determined to get it. If Hilary could walk fifty miles to find a school, I could find the money to build it.

NYAKA PRIMARY SCHOOL

Nyaka school officially opened in 2003 to 55 students, all **HIV/AIDS** orphans.

As attendance at Nyaka Primary School increased, the program built additional classrooms. All students are provided with free tuition, school supplies, uniforms, and shoes. Nyaka Primary teaches nursery through Primary-7, the equivalent of preschool through elementary school.

The Pioneer class of Nyaka Primary School graduated in 2008. Twenty-one of the 22 graduates passed their national exams. These students would be sponsored to attend secondary and vocational schools in the region. The first class of students graduated from high school December 2014. Fourteen students received high school diplomas. Twelve applied to universities.

CHAPTER 2

JUST BUILD IT

The Nyaka Project could not afford travel expenses early on, but I made sure to visit Uganda once a year on my own. In November 2006, after a twenty-hour journey from Detroit via Amsterdam, I arrived at Entebbe International Airport. That night I stayed at the Fang Fang Hotel in Kampala. The next day I rented a Land Cruiser and packed it full of gifts, including raised bread, one of Maama's favorite treats, and sweeties for the kids.

The journey to the village took another eight hours. Roads leaving Kampala are paved and in relatively good condition, but the farther one gets from the city, the more hazardous the driving. Rukungiri was the last town with electricity and good pavement. From there I descended the winding dirt road into the Enengo Gorge, crossed the river on the only metal bridge for miles, and goaded the rental up a steep incline on the other side.

Kambuga always seemed so large when I was a child, but the main part of town is a single dirt road lined with shops selling everything from hardware and building supplies to fresh produce and mattresses. Compared to American towns it feels tiny.

Nyakagyezi is a short drive from Kambuga on a rutted road. My first night is always spent with family and friends. We eat and drink and catch up with news and gossip. Work begins the next morning. Days are filled with meetings with students, teachers, volunteers, and community members. On this trip, I would also call on a few families that hosted Nyaka students.

The first family lived on the hillside along Kyabu Stream, which empties into the Birira River at the bottom of the Enengo Gorge. Nyakagyezi area has little level land. Most farms are located on steep slopes between hills.

I had barely started my descent when the path became impassable. Rather, I should say the path *looked* impassable. But there is always a way. Avoiding sharp rocks, I scooted along the edge of a gully and pressed on. Later I was forced to divert around an avocado tree and claw through some brush.

I came to a clearing in front of a mud daub house with a rusted iron roof. A boy on the stoop saw me and ran inside. A middle-aged woman holding a baby came out.

"*Agandi*," I said. "Is this the home of Kyarisima Jaqueline?"

"Yes," she said so quietly I barely heard. An older man with a floppy brown hat rounded the corner of the house.

"*Agandi*," he said.

"*Nigye.*" I shook his callused hand. "I am Director Kaguri."

"Mmm." He nodded. "You have come about Kyarisima? I am her uncle."

At fifteen, Kyarisima was one of the oldest students at Nyaka. She struggled in class and could not pass her exams. Her uncle had threatened to take her out of school if she was not promoted to Primary-6 this year. Kyarisima desperately wanted to remain.

"I am making home visits," I said.

He scratched his chin. "Kyarisma is failing."

"She is having difficulty with her studies, but we are not giving up."

"School is wasted on a child like her," he said. "She can stay home and work. She can cook and clean and take care of my children."

I tensed. Like many uncles forced into responsibility, he was making plans to marry her off. Families often see orphans as a burden rather than an asset, an extra mouth to feed, someone who may die of HIV/AIDS as their parents did. I needed to change that belief.

"Some students do well with academic work," I said. "Others learn trade skills. We will teach her tailoring. She will have a skill and earn money to share with the family."

He tipped his hat back, looking interested at the mention of money.

"In a year, she will make shirts, pants, dresses," I said. "She can set up a shop in town. If she does well, she might even hire someone to work for her."

"Mmm," he said. "You will train her at Nyaka?"

"Yes, of course." The uncle invited me to join him for lunch, but I thanked him and said I had other families to visit.

The other two encounters were less troublesome. Their students were thriving, and the families appreciated the food they brought from the Nyaka gardens to help supplement their farm.

On the steep climb back to Nyakagyezi, I turned my attention to the new school. Nancy Colier and Melissa McCool from the New York City area had raised enough money to build a couple of classrooms, but we had no time to waste. The academic year in Uganda runs from January to December. It was already November.

If students were to receive instruction for an entire year, the classrooms had to be ready soon.

The drive to Nyakishenyi takes about two hours on sandy, winding roads. When I arrived, I found both local administrators and residents eager to discuss the school. They were so enthusiastic that one farmer lent us a building to use as temporary classrooms. District leaders provided an office.

I asked community adults and children what they wanted to name their new school. They chose *Kutamba,* which means "healer." The school would be the first step in healing the community after the death and suffering that had weighed so heavily on them since HIV/AIDS arrived. They chose green uniforms to symbolize traditional medicinal plants used for healing. The Nyaka staff in Uganda hired a headmaster and two teachers.

The first Monday in February 2007, Professor Mondo, along with my sister Christine and two Rotary volunteers, Claire and Barbara from Philadelphia, opened Kutamba Primary School to 61 students. We had made a commitment. I prayed we would find additional resources.

Many of our supporters have specific goals. The Stephen Lewis Foundation funds the Grandmother Project and general operations, Seed and Light, Inc. from Albuquerque donates seeds, and Rotarians focus on water projects. Established Friends of Nyaka groups would help build classrooms but it could take years for Kutamba to catch up to Nyaka.

Just before Kutamba opened, Carol Realini, whom I had met at the Global Giving contest at Stanford University, suggested her friend, Carol Auld, visit Nyaka School. Carol and her husband, Robert, were interested in supporting a charity project in Africa.

In April, Carol visited Nyakagyezi. I was confident she would be impressed by our students and programs, and she was. After six weeks of working at Nyaka School, I hoped she and Rob would also be interested in supporting Kutamba School.

They were not. Carol had not even visited Kutamba.

"Why start a second school when you haven't finished the first?" she said over the phone. "You'll spread yourself too thin and not be able to keep either project alive."

I did not argue with her but took the news in stride and trusted that God would open another door. Building Kutamba might be a mistake, but it was a mistake I had to make for the kids' sake. They would only be children once. If they did not get into school now, they were destined to a life of poverty.

That summer I took advantage of some small funding sources and got a good price on two acres of land near the temporary building. Not long after that I received a surprise call from Carol.

"How are you doing, Jackson?" I heard excitement in her voice.

"I am fine. How are you?"

"Fantastic. I just attended Stephen Lewis' talk at the Aspen Ideas festival. I don't think I understood the true need you have for schools in rural Africa."

Stephen is a very articulate and inspiring speaker. He tells it like it is and does not mince words when he speaks about 75 million children not being able to attend school, most of them girls. "The yearning is great," are his words that I remember most vividly.

"I want you to check your calendar," Carol said. "Let's talk about building Kutamba School."

"What!" I am sure the whole neighborhood heard me. "You want to help build Kutamba?"

"Yes, Jackson. When can we get together?"

In August, I flew to Denver to meet Carol for the first time. She was a thin, energetic woman with gray hair and a generous smile. She quickly adopted me, becoming my first Jewish mother.

As we discussed the specifics of building a school, I felt like I was dreaming. She talked about raising enough money to build the entire school at one time. Could this be possible? We made a preliminary budget that was larger than anything I had done for Nyaka: $90,000. How could she possibly raise so much?

Carol and Rob held their first Kutamba gathering at their home. It was a small group, only fifteen people including their next-door neighbors, Jeanne and Allan Parleman. "I'm not sure it's going to work," Carol told me, but she had promised that whatever was pledged, she and Rob would match dollar for dollar.

I was shocked to learn that the event raised about $45,000 in one weekend. I could barely contain my excitement. Not only were Rob and Carol generous people, they had generous friends.

NATUKUNDA DENIS

My name is Natukunda Denis, my mother is Nyinakiiza Jolly and my dad was James Kakunguru. I have five siblings one sister and four brothers. My dad died when I was one year old, I did not have access to his picture to see what he looked like. Life became so difficult for my mother to raise all the six children.

My mother became so strong and suffered a lot to raise us. She never got a single help from relatives. We grew not having relatives, but today the relatives show up for who we are today, offering no help still, instead needing help from us. When I graduated, I heard them saying that in our family we have someone with a degree. I just smiled only because they want to harvest where they never planted. I wonder what they want to harvest.

Due to the challenges my mother faced while providing us with basic needs while we were young, we decided to go and be slaves for rich people. Me and my brothers used to go and work for a rich man in our village called George Muyaga. He used to pay me shs. 500 a day for working morning to evening. During a single day I used to do multiple tasks such as weeding the banana plantation, taking his cows to drink water, collecting water for the family and before I left, I would first go to collect firewood. Unfortunately, he would not pay me after work, he would pay me after a week's interval. I kept on working for him and saved that little money. This helped to buy school uniform, books, pens and other scholastic materials to at least be in school despite being in a miserable situation. I found it difficult to put on shoes on that savings, I would walk anywhere barefooted. Life was not easy because everyone was so desperate about life.

Joining Nyaka was a such a blessing in my life because I stopped being a slave for everyone. Nyaka became everything I needed. I got all the scholastic materials such as books, uniform, pens, pencils, clothes, soap, toothpaste, shoe polish, jerry and many others. Surprisingly my first time to put on shoes, is when I was admitted in Nyaka. The following morning, I woke up at 5:00am to put on my shoes and went to Nyaka Primary School. And I believe if I was not in Nyaka, my feet would not have tasted shoes even now. I have never regretted being an orphan because I have everything I need and have a caring dad, Dr. Twesigye Jackson Kaguri. I really love him so much. He is the dad I have now.

As I was growing, I had never travelled up to enengo bridge but when I was joining Primary-6, Nyaka took my class to Kampala and I was excited to travel all this far. When we reached in Rukungiri, I thought it was Kampala and when we reached Mbarara I thought it was Kampala. When we reached Kampala, I thought I was in heaven. We had a dinner with Professor Mondo. After, we visited the River Nile, Bujagali falls and went to Entebbe International Airport. Nyaka you got me from this far to a sweet life. My family is so thankful that I am in Nyaka. My mother is so thankful for Nyaka because she is enjoying life now because I am there to give her whatever she needs. I believe she will be the happiest mom. Proud of her.

I went to Nyaka Primary School in 2003-2008 and

obtained a first grade of 11 aggregates. After, I went to Ishaka Adventist College for Ordinary level from 2009-2012 where I got second grade of 34 aggregates. After I went to Bishop Comboni College-Kambuga for advanced level. I was doing a combination of HED/SM. These subjects were History, Economics, Divinity and Sub math. I scored 15 points.

From 2015-2018 I went to Makerere University Business School and I did Bachelor of Business Administration for three years. I was excited to study from Kampala the Capital City of Uganda because in my life I wished to study from there. While in third year I specialized in Finance and the course was so fabulous. I graduated 17th January 2019 with second class upper degree of CGPA 3.74. I was excited graduating from Makerere University because I had no hopes of reaching this level in my life. I was excited mom was present on that day and a representative from Nyaka Aids Orphans Project, Jackie.

Currently am working in Nyaka Aids Orphans Project as Sponsor A Student Associate in Kanungu district. Am excited to be back home as I have to give back to Nyaka through my effort. Am single and I do not have a child.

Thank you so much Dad, Dr Twesigye Jackson Kaguri, for putting a fabulous smile on my face. Am so delighted to have you in my life.

Thank you, Country Director Jennifer Nantale, towards my achievement. Thank you everyone in Nyaka Aids Orphans Project through this journey of my education. Sincere thanks to my sponsors, well-wishers, donors and friends for providing everything I needed. Thank you so much Beautiful World Canada for your support from Advanced level up to University. Thank you so much Sara Dunkley for your wonderful effort towards my success. I love you Tj Kaguri, am so proud of you.

Regards,

Natukunda Denis

CHAPTER 3

MAKE IT WORK

When Nic was four, he joined me on the 20-hour journey from Detroit to Entebbe Airport. He was only four years old, but I wanted to give Beronda a break. She was working long hours and childcare would be one less thing for her to worry about.

Nic took the long flights in stride. *Cave Crunch* was his favorite video game at the time and that kept him busy for hours. When he grew tired of gaming, the flight attendants seemed happy to entertain him.

On the drive to the village he was fascinated by the never-ending variety of people, *boda bodas*, and animals along the highway. Even the speed bumps and ruts in the road were fun for a four-year-old who enjoyed bouncing in his seat.

The sun was below the horizon by the time we reached the village. Still, Nic recognized the school from photographs he had seen.

"Nyaka School," he said, pointing. "Mukaaka and Shwenkuru live here."

"Yes," I said. We passed the L-shaped building, now a

completed primary school with seven classrooms. In the morning, we would be greeted by 183 smiling students in purple Nyaka uniforms.

I continued a short way up the road and pulled into my parents' grassy yard. The single-story stucco house looked to be in good condition. The corrugated iron roof was holding up well. My parents were happy with the home I had constructed for them, but I hoped to afford a better one in the future, after Nyaka and Kutamba were taken care of.

Maama and Faida rushed out to greet us, followed by Faida's young son, Sam.

"*Buhorogye*!" Maama shouted. She wrapped her arms around me. "My son has finally returned. Praise the Lord."

"I'm going to see my cows," Nic said. He jumped from the land cruiser and ran around the side of the house like he had lived there his whole life. Sam followed. Nic is undoubtedly the only boy in Okemos, Michigan who owns *ente* in Uganda. They are gifts given to him over the years and taken care of by Taata.

"Where is Taata?" I asked.

Faida's eyes narrowed. "Probably bragging about his new school."

I nodded. Taata enjoyed the status Nyaka school gave him in the village. Now that we were building Kutamba in the area where he grew up, he claimed that school too. He had told Professor Mondo that he never went to school, but now he owned two.

I had come to terms with Taata in recent years. Though I could not always understand his motives, he had done the best with what life granted him. Maama had been nearly crippled by a kick from an ornery cow when she was younger. Taata was crippled by something else, something that kept him from being the generous man my elder brother, Frank, had been.

In the following days, I met with teachers, board members, women in the Grandmothers Program, and people from the surrounding area. We were joined by Margaret Wright and Aissatou Diajhate from the Stephen Lewis Foundation who had come to monitor the Nyaka program.

I was impressed by Margaret's passion for community-based organizations. She understood that people were resilient, but it would take a concentrated effort to heal the deep wounds developed over thirty years. Aissatou was born and raised in Senegal. Being at Nyaka was like coming home for her. She danced with grannies and mentored girls.

Near the end of my visit, I drove with Nic, Margaret, and Aissatou through the winding hills that Hilary had walked earlier that year. It was finally time to see Kutamba first-hand. Our work had barely begun, but already I felt a sense of pride that one boy's journey had ignited this project. A single person *can* make a difference in this world.

The temporary building was located at the edge of a slope. From the outside, it resembled a log cabin. The interior featured plank walls. Small, glassless windows protected by shutters admitted light. The classrooms were dim, but better than no classrooms at all.

"*Agandi,*" the school headmaster said.

"*Nigye.*"

We met the local management committee and teachers, and I was finally able to introduce myself to Hilary. At 11, he was older than the other students, but he was getting his education. That was what mattered.

Like Nyaka, Kutamba has an anti-AIDS choir. The students

performed for us in the school yard. One boy kept the beat with a drum. Other children sang in Rukiga about *slim*, the Ugandan name for **HIV/AIDS**.

> *"Mighty, be mighty everyone.*
> *I thank everyone who has come*
> *Sit down and I'll tell*
> *About slim"*

One of the older girls stepped forward and told her personal story of how **AIDS** had affected her. Though *slim* had destroyed her parents and many in the community, "one person has come to rescue us." She smiled at me.

It made me self-conscious to hear such praise, but I only nodded and smiled back. My role as *The Director* was an important part of the local story, I suspected. As these students got to know me, hopefully they would come to see me more as a benevolent uncle who loves and supports them without condition.

The girl added that all people must work together to beat **AIDS** and restore peace, love, and community. Everyone clapped and the students repeated their song. Several more students stepped forward to tell their own stories.

Afterward, we drove to see the property for the new Kutamba buildings. It was large enough to house a school, but construction was going to be a challenge. In Michigan, this land would have made a great sledding hill.

We had been fortunate to find a flat location for Nyaka School. We built without creating terraces and sloped driveways. But most of rugged western Uganda is not level. Farms and homes are cut into the hillsides, one reason that *embuzi* are a preferred farm animal. They traverse uneven land much easier than *ente*.

"Are you going to be able to build here?" Margaret asked.

"It will take a lot of engineering," I conceded. There was not a single level area on the plot. The budget that had seemed so abundant at the time, might not be enough. "We will figure it out."

The remainder of my visit was less stressful. I enjoyed long evenings of conversation with family and friends in the dim light of a paraffin lantern and taking my morning run along the grass paths that passed banana plantations, avocado trees weighted with fruit, and vegetable gardens. We celebrated with roasted goat meat, steamed *matooke*, peanut sauce, and greens. The days were sunny and warm, the nights filled with stars.

And then it was time to return to the U.S.

In November, Indiana Friends of Nyaka held their annual banquet in Bloomington, one of several events throughout the country that provided ongoing support for our Nyaka programs. This, however, was the group that launched us. They believed in our vision from the very beginning and I felt honored to attend despite the ongoing pressures of getting Kutamba School off the ground. Also, this year was special because Professor Mondo had traveled from Kampala to speak.

David Brenner began the evening with a benediction, then introduced Brittany Linville. Each year a volunteer or visitor to Nyaka speaks about their experience. Brittany described her stay at Nyaka School. Using a slideshow, she introduced the audience to many of the kids.

"I've never seen students work so hard, be so eager to learn, or be so appreciative," she said. "Some of them walk two hours each way to school. I came home and saw all my stuff, and I started crying. Why do I need all of this?"

Professor Mondo spoke next, and though he did not use the fruits of technology, he made his point firmly and well. Donations made at this gathering were being put to responsible use and the projects were making a meaningful difference in the region and the country. He told me privately that he was pleased to find such support in the United States. It was a testament to my leadership. I thanked him and smiled, but inside I knew the truth. Success in this project was primarily a testament to our kids. They had experienced suffering and deprivation and now were seeing what education and connection to the greater world could bring. They would become agents of positive change, I had no doubt. Already many of our students vowed to return to the village after their education and help lift their community. Doctors, nurses, accountants, agricultural agents, truck drivers, tailors. Nyakagyezi needed them all.

As I was moving along the buffet, I felt a tug on my sleeve. I turned to find a blond-haired girl.

"Do you remember me, Mr. Jackson?"

"Of course, I do," I said. Earlier in the year, I had visited the First Methodist Church in Martinsville, Indiana, where I met the Northerns and their seven-year-old daughter. She was very sweet and concerned for the Nyaka children. "How are you, Cameron?"

Cameron grinned and looked back at her mother, who nodded encouragingly.

"I asked my parents if I could give my piggy bank money to Nyaka. I wrote letters to my family and friends. They gave me money for Nyaka. It's back at our table." She looked over her shoulder toward a jar sitting on a banquet table. The jar was filled with coins, bills and checks. "I have $868.48."

"Wow," I said, genuinely impressed. "That is wonderful."

Her grin grew. "I told them that their change and my change could make a difference!"

"It will," I said. "That is a lot of money."

"I'm going to raise money every year."

I nodded. "I am certain that you will." And, in fact, she has.

The evening was a great success. A local entrepreneur, Whitney Gates, capped it off with a large pledge in his mother's name.

In less than three weeks, I was off again. Carol and Rob were holding a second fundraiser for Kutamba. Despite it being the Christmas weekend, I left Beronda and Nic alone for the holiday. Kutamba must come first.

Rob met me at the Durango Airport and drove us along a four-lane highway through desert scrub lands. I did not see a tree for miles. Always, the mountains were in the distance. These were not the steep hills of Uganda, covered in banana plantations and tea farms, but rocky protrusions shawled with snow and blued by distance.

I did not comprehend how *much* snow until we started the climb to Aspen. Snow everywhere, two, three, four feet deep, more snow than I had seen in my life. As we drew closer to town, I noticed ski trails carved through the evergreens like pure white streams down the mountainsides.

Aspen was crowded. People strolled the sidewalks in ski coats of every color with stylish hats and pants to match. There must have been a hundred shops. I had read that ski slopes brought millions of dollars from visiting tourists. What would the people of Nyakagyezi think? Many were lucky to have one pair of shoes. These people probably spent more money on a pair of shoes than it costs to send a student to a secondary boarding school for a year.

I felt a moment of irritation, but only that. It was not these men and women who were wicked, but the systems of the world that make such inequalities commonplace.

Rob and Carol's home was nestled in a residential neighborhood not unlike my own. The house appeared small at first glance, with carved wood trim and a Victorian-style tower. On one side a wall of windows opened onto a great room, giving it a more modern appearance. When I entered, I discovered the house extended back onto their property and was much larger than I had thought.

Carol welcomed me with a hug. "*Agandi*, Jackson. Did you have a good flight? I'm sure you're tired. Have you eaten?" Only their three boys were home for the holidays, so I was welcomed to stay in their daughter's room.

The fundraiser was held both Saturday and Sunday evenings. Over one-hundred people attended in all. Rob assured them that he and Carol had been to Nyaka and that the money was going to a good cause. For those who still doubted, he informed them that Nyaka had asked him to audit their books since he was a retired VP from Fidelity Investments.

Those two nights became a blur of names, faces, and promises. Some pledged hundreds, others, thousands. Rob's brother-in-law gave $10,000. Carol Realini and her husband, Joe Tumminaro, and Diane and Bill Hunkler each pledged $5,000. By the end of the weekend, we had the rest of the money to build Kutamba. I was astonished.

"That was more than I expected," Carol said. I said a silent prayer. Instead of railing against the systems of the world earlier, I should have thanked God for granting us compassion.

The problem now was figuring out how to build a school on

that hill. At least it was not as steep as the terrain surrounding Aspen. Maybe we should open a ski school instead. The thought of children whooshing down a slope in Kutamba-green ski jackets made me smile, and the worry was gone. We would use the land we had. We would make it work.

ARIHIHI RONALD

Great appreciation goes to Nyaka project foundation for continuous support and eye monitoring that was put on me towards my social and academic success. It has been a great war since 2003 when I started my primary education at Nyaka Primary School until 2018 when I graduated with my first Bachelor's Degree within the same system. The momentous struggle continues as I take this chance to thank Nyaka on behalf of the almighty GOD for helping me from the suffering of being an orphan to the life of being a great responsible person.

I completed my education on 6th July 2018 and went to face the world's life expectance. Since then, life has always been good as am trying to figure out how to make myself better. I am now competent doing a side job which deals with making stoves, and this business helps to meet the house rent and other sustainability as I live in Kampala.

CHAPTER 4

GROWING PAINS

Michigan in winter is about as far removed from Uganda as any place could be. I was trapped in short, dark days filled with cold and snow while most of my family basked in 85-degree heat and 12-hour daylight. Still, I was happy for the most part. Work on Kutamba school moved ahead so quickly I could barely believe it. The Aulds had not only raised enough money to build a school, but Carol had discovered an architect at the Aspen for Ideas Festival to create it for that impossible slope of land.

Matthew Miller was from Architecture for Humanity, a global organization that designs structures for disadvantaged communities. Their buildings use renewable energy systems and local materials and methods. Matt was a good architect despite his colorful use of language—one of the workers informed me later he had learned the phrase, "what the fuck," from Matt without knowing its meaning. I had to tell him that was not appropriate to use around our visitors from America.

Members of the Indiana Friends of Nyaka and Sherwood Oaks Church under the direction of Pastor Brad Pontius flew to Uganda in late January. They joined up with Carol and Rob in Kampala.

On February 3rd, the group traveled to Nyakishenyi to break ground for the new Kutamba School. Despite news that the guest of honor, Professor Mondo Kagonyera, could not attend for health reasons, a large crowd gathered. Building a new school was an historic event that attracted everyone in the area. Students proudly wore their new uniforms—girls in green dresses, boys in green shirts and black pants. I remained in Michigan but was informed of the events later.

Mukaakas sang their traditional welcome song, prompting two Americans to join them in the *okutagurura*, a fast-paced Kikiga dance. It was apparently a joyful spectacle to behold *bazungu* attempting the jumps and swaying-arm movements.

After the dance, Pastor Pontius prayed for God to bless the land on which the school was to be built. Carol and Rob were invited to break ground, and the pastor laid the first brick.

Boney Biryatuyita, the Nyakishenyi Council Chairperson, praised the U.S. team. "Because of your good will and mercy," he said, "the children of Nyakishenyi are going to benefit greatly from Kutamba School."

Later, the American group sat down to brainstorm ideas for contributing more to the Nyaka Fund. Pastor Pontius embraced the idea of setting up a coffee shop in Bloomington. A Ugandan-themed night could be held every month, and proceeds from each cup of coffee sold that day would go to Nyaka.

"We want our patrons to know they are buying a cup of coffee for a cause," Pastor Pontius later told me. "Their time and money will change lives in Uganda."

"It is a wonderful concept," I agreed.

The Pourhouse opened in 2008 with the goal of donating 100

percent of profits and tips to charity. The large space had plenty of room for Indiana University students to stop by for a cup of coffee, a casual date, or an extended study session. There was even a small stage for live music.

At that time, six churches were supporting Nyaka with special collections: United Presbyterian Church, Bloomington, Indiana; Sacred Heart Parish, Farmington, New Mexico; Led by the Spirit of God Church. Little Rock, Arkansas; Faith Missionary Church, Martinsville, Indiana; Seventh Day Adventist Church, Big Rapids, Michigan; and Sherwood Oaks Christian Church, Bloomington, Indiana.

Sherwood Oaks Church made monthly contributions to the Nyaka Fund and provided $5,000 to purchase a school van. The church also conducted teacher-training courses for Kutamba and Nyaka teachers to equip them with better computer skills.

When Pastor Pontius and several Sherwood Oaks members returned to Uganda, we welcomed them as family and made every effort to strengthen the bond between us. As a non-denominational church, they seemed a good fit for Nyaka, which accepted students of any religion.

You can imagine my surprise when longtime Nyaka supporter, Otto Ray, called a month later. "The church elders voted to stop donating to Nyaka."

"Why? I thought everyone enjoyed their stay. Brad laid the cornerstone for Kutamba last time he was there."

"We had a wonderful time," Otto said. "It was life-changing. Brad and the other visitors are as surprised as I am. And angry too."

"What happened?"

"Someone mentioned seeing a Muslim girl attending Nyaka School."

"Nyaka accepts orphans of all religions," I said. "We have Muslims on our school board."

"I know," Otto said. "But one of the church elders insists Sherwood Oaks should only support Christians."

"Can Brad change their minds?" Brad Pontius is a persuasive orator.

"No," Otto said. "The elders have the final say."

I leaned back in my office chair. Were these elders unfamiliar with the parable of the Good Samaritan in *Luke 10:25-37?* In the story, a man is beaten and left beside the road. A Priest and a Levite, who should be the first to help an injured man, ignore him. A good Samaritan finally comes to his aid. The verse teaches us that neighbors are not only the people in our community, country, or congregation. All people are our neighbors. Our sympathy should extend to everyone.

I tried to accept Otto's news and move on but could not help feeling disappointed. It was a sad day.

That was not the only bad news. While Nyaka and Kutamba schools were growing, my marriage was dying from neglect. I cannot say I did not notice we were drifting apart. Beronda and I had busy careers. Some days we barely said hello to each other. I guess I thought it was the American way. Then, one day, it was over.

Beronda decided to move into an apartment, leaving me alone in our big house. Our separation was amicable, and we shared custody of Nic, but I suddenly went from family man to single father. And I carried all the guilt and embarrassment that went with it.

When I spoke with my parents on the phone, I chose not to mention the separation right away. No doubt Taata would remind me more than once how he had advised me to marry a village girl.

Except for my time with Nic, I buried myself in work, scouring the country for donors. With two schools, we would soon have twice the students, twice the cost for food and supplies, twice the number of families to support, and a larger Grandmothers Program. I could not expect more from the Aulds. They had already gone above and beyond.

I began to embrace the weather and even resented when spring rolled around with its bright leaves and warm rain. The gloom of long winter days seemed appropriate for this time in my life

KOMUHANGI IRENE

My name is Komuhangi Irene and am 24 years old. I have one baby boy and his name is Kiziito Aaron. I am married to Mr. Kiziito Dennis though not legally married but thinking about it. He graduated from Kyambogo university with bachelor's degree in computer science and technology and is currently working with the civil aviation, Uganda.

My father was Mubandizi Julius and my mother was Chance Jackeline. Both died of Aids. My mother died first. She died when I was two years old and my youngest brother still breast feeding. I have one big sister and one young brother am a second born. My father died when I was four years old and from there, we started living a miserable life.

After my parents' deaths we all started staying with our grandmother and grandfather who are residents of Ngaram village and Kayanga cell. They never had enough money to afford all the basic needs we needed as children due to the fact that my brother needed too much care and attention, but I thank the almighty GOD our guardians managed to take good care of us. They couldn't manage everything but at least they tried because none of us got malnourished. They provide to us things like food, soap, clothes but could not manage to pay for our school fees and even afford all the scholastic materials. One day I was with my grandfather and we were coming from church when we meant a certain lady who told us a school for orphans they were planning to open in Nyakagyezi. The following morning, we had to wake up very early and start the journey. We reached the school at around 9 o'clock and found Teacher Lydia, who was able to register and told us to wake up very early in morning the following Monday and come to school. Me and my brother plus my grandmother went home happily. We could not wait for Monday to arrive.

When we reached home and my grandmother told one of my uncles about the school and how we were admitted, he thought she was lying. He even shouted and said it's just a waste of time, that my grandmother never had enough to do that's why she spent the whole day in Nyakagyezi. Slowly by slowly he started believing through seeing the things the school would give us.

I finished Primary-7 from Nyaka Primary School, went to Ishaka Adventist college where I finished my Ordinary level, and later to Bishop Comboni College Kambuga where I finished my advanced level respectively. I went to Kyambogo University and graduated with bachelor's in social and community development. I am now working with the Nyaka Aids Orphans Program as a school social worker.

I extend my sincere thanks to the founder of Nyaka aids orphans project Mr. Jackson Kaguri for the kind heart he has to help orphans and other people. I never had hopes of studying but he managed to give me free education with all the free scholastic materials I can't really thank him enough, but I pray to the almighty God to bless him and add him many more years. More so I thank the donors for the support they are giving Nyaka we are very grateful. And lastly, I thank all the Nyaka family for the good work they are doing in Nyaka and for the smooth running of the project.

Thank You That's my story.

CHAPTER 5

A SMALL FISH IN A LARGE LAKE

With the new Kutamba buildings scheduled to open in January 2009, it became apparent that I needed to approach a large funding source, something like the Clinton Global Initiative (CGI). I looked on-line, but their annual meeting was by invitation only.

Once again, Carol Auld came to the rescue. Her daughter had been a roommate with Chelsea Clinton at Stanford University, and they were still good friends. I could not believe the coincidence, which was probably no coincidence. By now in this journey, I understood that God intervenes at the appropriate time in the appropriate way. All it took was a phone call to get me registered.

The annual meeting was a three-day affair in September 2008. I started preparing months ahead, scheduling vacation time from my MSU job, finding a place to stay in New York City, trying to think of what to say to prospective donors. I would truly be a small fish in a large lake, but when would I have another chance like this? The flight from Detroit is short, but that day I was so anxious it seemed to take forever.

One of our most faithful donors, Deborah Delmer, had invited me to stay in her home. Deborah is an energetic woman with dark, curly hair. A couple of years before we built Nyaka School, she left her position as chair of the Section of Plant Biology at the University of California Davis and joined the Rockefeller Foundation to evaluate programs aimed at crop improvement. She soon became Associate Director for Food Security. She had been elected to the National Academy of Sciences in 2004 while assessing genetically modified crops to determine if they could be used in African countries. It was her interest in Uganda that brought her to us.

In 2005, Deborah's daughter, Sara, signed up to volunteer for three months. She helped with our water program and later became a member of our Board of Advisors.

Deborah's home is not far from the Natural History Museum, Central Park, and the Sheraton Hotel where the CGI meeting was being held. I jogged around Central Park's lake in the early morning before the city got too hot.

It had been years since I had arrived in New York to attend Columbia University. Things had not changed much. As in Kampala, people, taxis, buses, and cars were everywhere, only New York did not have red dust covering everything. There were no *boda boda* drivers weaving in and out of traffic and widows did not roost on every corner selling bags of dried beans, jewelry, and other items to support themselves.

After my run, I dressed and ate a delicious breakfast. On my way out the door, I straightened my tie and tried not to look nervous. Deborah and her husband, gracious hosts that they were, wished me luck. I was glad she was confident in my abilities. I felt overwhelmed.

Security at the hotel was tight. The Clinton meeting coincided with the UN General Assembly, and all the heavy hitters were in town. Men with suits and dark glasses followed them everywhere. Little wires looped over the security guards' ears. I did not see guns, but they surely had them hidden beneath those formal jackets.

No one stopped me, which surprised me a bit. In my good suit, I must have looked official enough to belong. I followed a group of women down a set of steps past the main desk and stopped at a cluster of tables manned by young people. I received a name badge and a packet that contained a conference agenda booklet, a duffle bag, Toms shoes, and other handouts.

The CGI event had booked the entire hotel and numerous seminars would take place simultaneously in dozens of meeting rooms. There were working group luncheons and dinners, and an information exchange in the Metropolitan Ballroom. The Plenary session would feature Lance Armstrong, with Bill Clinton and Al Gore also speaking. Kofi Annan, President George H. W. Bush, Barack Obama, Tony Blair, Nobel Peace Prize winner Mohammad Yunus, Bill Gates and Kanye West were listed as attendees. I could not believe I would be in a room with all of these famous people.

The wide hall was carpeted, its circular patterns blending with the tan shade of the walls, chairs and benches. Everything was neat and positioned exactly. What was I doing here? I was a boy from the highlands of western Uganda. Growing up, I wore my brother's hand-me-downs. My parents had never been in a building over one story tall. How could I speak with these people? They were some of the most powerful dignitaries on the planet, used to dealing with world affairs.

The auditorium was as opulent as the rest of the hotel, its stage complete with red velvet curtains. CGI signs glowed against a blue backdrop with white stars. President Clinton spoke about the looming economic emergency, global warming, and how we should deal with the world's current and future problems.

"This is a group of really gifted people," he said.

After several more speeches, meeting leaders encouraged people to network in breakout sessions. Working groups that day included Global Health, Environment and Climate Change, Poverty Alleviation, and Education. Nyaka's mission fit into three of the four.

I do not even remember which I chose, but CEOs from Save the Children, Oxfam, and World Vision were represented. As the afternoon progressed, some organizations made major deals, and these were announced over the public-address system. I kept to myself, too intimidated to speak up.

Later in the day, Richard Branson and Oprah Winfrey took the stage. I felt smaller and smaller. By dinner time, I was exhausted. I could not see how any of these people would be interested in helping two small schools in western Uganda.

As the taxi transported me back to Deborah's house, I considered not returning the next day. Juilliard School and Lincoln Center passed by my window. I gazed blankly at the traffic surrounding us, so many people going about their busy lives. I truly was a minnow here. CGI donors were looking for million-dollar organizations.

At Deborah's house, I took a deep breath. Carol and Sara had gone to a lot of trouble to get me an invitation. I should not be so ungrateful. Even if the Nyaka organization was too small to benefit from the conference, I could use this meeting as a learning experience.

The next day, I spotted Chelsea Clinton standing beside her

parents and mustered up the courage to introduce myself.

"Hello," I said, extending my hand. "I am Jackson Kaguri, a friend of Rob and Carol Auld."

"Oh, hi," Chelsea said. "Sara told me about you." She turned to President Bill Clinton. "Daddy, this is Jackson. He's friends with Sara's parents."

"Hello, Jackson," the president said with his southern drawl. He took my hand. "Pleasure to meet you. What organization are you here with?"

I think I said Nyaka AIDS Orphans School and that I was from Uganda. Secretary of State, Hillary Clinton, turned to greet me, and then before I knew it, I was walking away. I looked down at my hand. I had just met a president of the United States of America. No one was going to believe it back home.

As the meetings continued, I became so disoriented that at one point I actually sat down by myself at a table in the dining area, which is not proper etiquette. Fundraisers should always be interacting with others at an event, but I felt so out of place that I needed to rest and regroup.

I was not alone for long. As the salad was being served, an older couple approached the table. He was a white man with receding hair and glasses, and she a Filipino woman with reddish-blond hair and a friendly smile.

"Are these seats saved?" the man asked.

"No," I said with relief. "Please, sit."

He held the chair for the woman and seated himself beside me.

"I'm Barry Segal," he said, shaking my hand. "And this is my wife, Dolly."

"I am Jackson Kaguri. I am here with the Nyaka AIDS Orphans Project."

A server placed a salad dish in front of Mr. Segal.

"Where's Nyaka?" he asked.

I told him we were based in western Uganda. "We have one primary school in Nyakagyezi with 206 students and another being completed in Nyakishenyi with 93 students." Speaking much too fast, I ran through our entire program, including two water systems, a gardening program, breakfast and lunch programs, two full-time nurses, HIV/AIDS education with an anti-AIDS choir, and a developing Grandmothers Program.

"Nyaka must be near Rwanda," he said.

"Yes. The school is very close to the border."

"I've been to Rwanda to visit the Aghozo-Shaolom Youth Village overseen by Ann Heyman," he said. "Do you know Ann? She's attending the conference."

"No," I said. "I must meet her."

I immediately relaxed. Here was someone who had been to eastern Africa and had seen firsthand the devastation AIDS and the Rwandan civil war had brought. When I spoke of the rugged hills, and the children with threadbare clothes and no shoes who were anxious to go to school, he understood. He saw the children's potential.

"I am impressed that you serve both the children and the grandmothers," he said.

"We want our orphans to have a normal home experience and not be institutionalized. Since *mukaakas* care for most orphans, it makes sense to support them both."

We continued speaking, but I did not tell Mr. Segal of my lack of success connecting with donors. I was embarrassed to admit that I was lost at an event of this caliber and magnitude.

He leaned across the table. "I understand how hard it is to raise money," he said. "I have supported a number of organizations like yours."

"You have?" Mr. Segal was such a personable man that I had forgotten he might also be a donor. My heart raced. Was he considering Nyaka?

"Here's the deal," he said, handing me a napkin and pen. "Give me your mailing address. Next week I will send you a check for $10,000. If you use it well and account for it, I will give you more. If you don't, I will consider the offer finished and you won't hear from me again."

For a moment I thought this was the biggest joke ever. Was someone filming me? How could a stranger come up and offer $10,000? The money would go a long way in helping supply Kutamba with books, uniforms, teachers' salaries and other supplies. I filled out my office address on the napkin. Never have I had to concentrate so hard to keep my writing legible.

After lunch, Mr. and Mrs. Segal each handed me a card. *B and D Holdings*. I later learned more about this power couple. Barry Segal is an extraordinary man who owned an industrial roofing company called **BRADCO** for 40 years. With six grown children and his wife, Dolly, working at his side, he is a force of change in the world.

Barry sold his company in 2006 to ABC stores, the same year he met the equally amazing Ann Heyman. Ann had started an organization called Aghahoza Shalom Village in Rwanda to care for vulnerable children left behind after the 1994 genocide. She invited Barry to Rwanda.

He was moved by the plight of children and fell in love with Ann's mission. That led to him building the **Barry Segal Learning Center** at Agahoza and founding the nonprofit Segal Family

Foundation. Since then, he has become friends with other men and women from the continent including Dikembe Mutombo in the Democratic Republic of the Congo (DRC), Kip Keno in Kenya, and MacDella Cooper in Liberia. A passionate advocate for population control and health, he also founded Focus on Health.

"It was a pleasure to meet you, Mr. Segal."

"Barry," he said. "Call me Barry."

I floated through the rest of the conference. Thoughts of that $10,000 check swirled through my mind. What would be the best use for it? Paying teachers? School supplies? A dining hall?

Bill Clinton gave the closing speech. I wondered if I would hear from Mr. Segal—Barry—again. Would the check really arrive in the mail, or would our small program be forgotten amid this high-powered event? Barry had been very business-like and to the point, but I had only just met him.

I soon found that he was a man of his word. His check arrived in the mail a few days later. The donation gave us the cushion we needed to open Kutamba school with all the teachers and supplies we needed for the first three primary classes.

In January 2009, students were greeted by their teachers and filed into their new Kutamba classrooms. I thanked God. I never thought I would see an entire school building completed in two years' time. I also promised myself we would not get involved with more building projects until Kutamba's operations were completely supported. Construction had gone well, but the stresses had been nearly unbearable.

KUTAMBA PRIMARY SCHOOL

A boy named Hilary walked over 50 miles by himself after hearing there was a school where HIV/AIDS orphans could attend for free. The Nyaka Program decided to build Kutamba Primary School in his community. In 2007, students attended a temporary school until Kutamba officially opened in 2009.

Unlike Nyaka, Kutamba was built in only two years.

Kutamba officially opened in 2009. Twenty-nine students graduated in 2012. They joined thirty Nyaka Primary School graduates and 15 Secondary School graduates.

CHAPTER 6

FOR WANT OF A BOOK

Now that we had two schools to support, I was on a never-ending quest for funding. That meant attending every possible event where I could spread the word about the Nyaka Program.

East Lansing is an old town, and the neighborhoods along Michigan Avenue near Sparrow Hospital are tree-lined and quiet. *Everybody Reads Books and Stuff,* owned by Scott Harris, is a bookstore located along the avenue amid a cluster of shops and restaurants. I was invited by Nyaka supporters to attend a reading group that was discussing the *Poisonwood Bible,* which takes place in the DRC. They thought I would be interested.

The DRC extends along Uganda's western border, cutting Lake Albert and Lake Edward in half. Much of the area is mountainous, but the mountains do not deter the passage of goods and, unfortunately, armed rebels and troops.

The DRC's history mirrors Uganda's. It was a kingdom before being colonized by Belgium in the 19th century. Rubber plantations became the sites of murder and torture. Finally, in 1960, citizens rebelled and established their independence. For many years, the country remained unstable because tribal leaders were much more powerful than the central government. Eventually, Mobutu Sese Seko took command and united the country until the late 1990s when Rwanda invaded. This led to the First Congo War. A second war followed in 1998 which involved both Rwanda and Uganda. That ended in 2003, but the western border became a hiding place for Allied Democratic Forces (ADF).

Nyakagyezi is not far from that border. I suppose I should have been more worried when I built the school, but I am a man of hope. Uganda had survived Idi Amin's brutal dictatorship. My grandfather had been imprisoned for his religious beliefs. But we survived. The worst times were behind us. Uganda was moving forward, and I saw more promise than desperation.

A young man with a round face, glasses, and ball cap greeted me as I entered the bookstore. "Hi. I'm Chris Singer. You must be Jackson. I'm glad you could come." He led me to a group of mostly women gathered in a circle, books on their laps. I chose a chair near the door and opened a copy of the book I had received from my dear friend, Harriet Lewis.

The novel is set in 1959. One of the characters, Anatole, is an orphan who becomes a schoolteacher. I could see why the group thought I would be interested. As the story progresses, a Baptist minister arrives with his family to save the souls of the lowly Africans. When someone in the group suggested the minister's garden failed because he knew nothing of local agriculture, I could not help but speak up.

"This is still a problem today. We often deal with foreign organizations that do not fully understand what they are proposing. They have good intentions, but they arrive with preconceived notions. They do not think to ask the people what they need."

I explained that Nyaka is a comprehensive program designed to lift both the kids and the community out of poverty. In this regard it is different from many programs. Foreign aid that supplies food or medicines is a temporary fix that does not address underlying problems in the villages. Providing books for a school is fine, but who will pay for tuition and teachers? Organizations come and go, putting a Band-Aid on the wound, but not truly helping the people to heal themselves.

By the end of the meeting, I felt comfortable with the group. Chris was extremely interested in hearing more about Nyaka.

"My concern is with social justice," he said. "Deb and I have started a network of people here in town who are interested in world issues. I'd love to meet with you sometime and find out more about your human rights work and the Nyaka program."

"Sure." I gave him my card. "Call me."

On the drive home, I tried to imagine book groups in Nyakagyezi. First, we would need books. Most people in the village did not own any. The schools usually had only textbooks. My own family had possessed only one book when I was growing up, the *Baibuli Erikwera,* the Holy Bible written in in our local language, Rukiga.

As a boy, I was more curious than most. One of my obsessions was sneaking into my parents' room to see the *Baibuli.* Our house only had three rooms: a living area and two bedrooms. Kitchens are built separately in the village to keep smoke out of the main house. Latrines are usually located at the back of one's property. Constructed of mud-daub with only a few small windows, the house was always dim. My parents' room was even darker.

We children slept on mats on the packed-dirt floor of our

room. Maama and Taata had a wooden bed frame with crisscrossing ropes to keep their mats off the dirt. The gap beneath gave Maama a place to store what little she owned, including the black, leather-bound *Baibuli*.

When I was very young, I would make sure Maama was busy outside, then creep into the room and peer at the mysterious book with its splayed-out pages smudged from overuse. Sometimes I would touch the cover and run my fingers over the embossed title. More often than not, she discovered my snooping.

"Twesi," Maama would call. "Where are you?"

"Here, Maama." I would rush to the backyard where she was preparing steamed *matooke* and beans or some other delicious meal in the kitchen building.

"What were you doing?" She would look at me out of the corner of her eye and add sticks to the fire.

"Nothing, Maama."

"You know the rules. You are not to touch the *Baibuli*."

"Yes, Maama." I swear she had some secret connection to that book.

As I grew older, Friday became my favorite day. Each week, the Seventh Day Adventist Church assigns a lesson to congregations around the world for the Saturday Sabbath. It does not matter whether we are in Michigan, Uganda, France, or the Philippines, we do the same lesson.

Maama read the *Baibuli* almost every day, but on Friday she would carry it outside and sit under the tree near the goat pen to study the assigned scriptures. Christine and Faida helped her while I watched raptly, hoping to have my own *Baibuli* someday.

Increasingly, I was able to avoid Maama's detection and took greater chances with the *Baibuli*. One of the best times for sneaking was when she was working in the garden. The vegetables were far enough away that I even dared to carry the book out of the house. The mango tree in the side yard provided shade and cover. I looked up lessons we were being taught at church.

On one excursion, this was *Ezekiel 20:20* near the back of the Old Testament. I could have turned to the passage directly but enjoyed the feel of the pages between my fingers. I took my time, glancing through *Joshua* and *Samuel* and *Psalms*, remembering other stories I had heard at church.

When I reached *Ezekiel*, I read out loud. "Kandi mugume mweze sabato zangye, zibe akamanyiso ahagati yangye naimwe, mubone kumanya ku nyowe Mukama ndi Runganga waanyu." *Hallow my Sabbaths; and they shall be a sign between me and you, that ye may know that I am the Lord your God.*

I had no trouble reading in school even when we learned English, Uganda's state language. Reading at school was interesting, but not as compelling as the stories in the *Baibuli*. *They shall be a sign between me and you.* I felt God was talking directly to me. He was there for me when I needed him. I only had to read his words and pray.

I perused the lesson again and again, memorizing each word. Other kids at church would be surprised I remembered it so well when it was time to recite. My goal was also to write it. I traced my fingers over the words.

Our other lesson was *Exodus 20:8*. "Ijuka kwesa ekiro kya sabato." *Remember the Sabbath day, keep it holy.* I promised myself I would do that always. When I was a grown man, I would have my own *Baibuli* just like Maama.

The goats staked in the backyard were my alarm system. A series of bleats warned me that Maama was coming. I closed the

Baibuli and rushed in the front door.

"Twesi," Maama called from behind the house.

"Yes, Maama." I tiptoed into the bedroom and placed the book under the bed, exactly as I had found it.

"Come here," she said.

"I am coming." She did not catch me that day or any day after that. At the time I thought I was clever. Looking back, I think Maama knew what I was up to all along.

Chris and Deb Singer were eager to help Nyaka. Initially, they volunteered their time, but I was eventually able to hire Chris to provide grant writing and public relations. He started the Michigan Friends of Nyaka to support the school.

While Chris was helping in Michigan, I received an email from Stephen Lewis' daughter, Ilana, who co-founded the Stephen Lewis Foundation with her father. Ilana is a labor and human rights lawyer who spent eight years at the United Nations Development Fund for Women. She has been active in assisting grassroots women's groups around the world, including our Grandmothers Program. I thought she was contacting me about the grandmothers, but the email concerned libraries.

> We had a couple reach out to us. Jim and Lynda
> Martin. They are funding libraries around the world.
> They wanted me to suggest an organization that
> could use a library and I thought Nyaka would be
> interested.

I had mentioned to Ilana that Susan Linville and I were writing a book about my life and the building of Nyaka School. I had plans to write other books specifically for the village children. It was important that they read books about people like themselves. A library would be a perfect fit.

I typed back:

> A library. It is just what the community needs. I am very interested.

Nic must have read 1,000 books by that point. I imagined Nyakagyezi kids and adults having a place with that many books to choose from, maybe more. It would be the first library in western Uganda. It would be a large building located next to the school. Not just a library, but a multimedia room for computers to link to the internet and a public meeting room for the community. *Dream big,* I thought. *Then make it happen.* Apparently, my vow to avoid future building projects was destined to have a short lifespan.

Ilana sent a follow-up email.

> I will put you in touch with Jim. You can discuss the project with him.

I did some research. The Martins, who were Canadian, called their foundation Blue Lupin Libraries, named for a flower that self-seeds. They believed literacy and learning would spread just like those seeds. Lynda was interested in libraries because they spurred the imagination. She wrote that *books are like the wind, they let the mind fly.* The Martins wanted their libraries to help people around the world fly, too. This made me even more excited to talk to Jim.

The discussion did not start well. Jim said that he and Lynda were building *one-room* libraries. My grand plans deflated. In the past I would have accepted a one-room library, but I had learned some important things at a strategic retreat in Mexico sponsored by Opportunity Collaboration, a global network of leaders dedicated to building sustainable solutions to poverty and injustice. They hold two four-day collaborative summits each year, one in the United States and one in Mexico. The meetings are all-inclusive and designed to help forge alliances and advance an organization's social impact.

Just because someone is offering to build something, does not mean you have to accept it, they stressed. Take only what is good for the organization.

Nyaka School had firsthand experience with that problem. Some years earlier, a donor had offered to build a basketball court. We did not really need a court. The kids play soccer and netball, not basketball. I said yes anyway. We received money to build a large cement court in the front yard of the school that could have been used for something we really needed, like a cafeteria. The recession hit around that time and the court was never finished. For years, it sat empty and unused, an important lesson.

"Nyaka is in need of a larger library," I said to Jim. "There are over 300,000 people in Kanungu District. We need a community library. That will take more than a single room."

"We've only built one-room libraries to this point," Jim said.

"Does that mean you cannot build a larger one?"

Jim hesitated.

"I think we will need four or five rooms," I said. "Reading rooms arranged according to age. A main lending library for the community. And I would like to have computer access and a conference room."

"I'll have to discuss this with Lynda," Jim said. "We'd need building plans and cost estimates. It would be a large venture."

"I will get the cost estimates for you," I said.

"Fine," he said. "We'll talk about this again."

I was encouraged that he did not reject the idea out of hand. In the following days I became determined to convince him and Lynda that the project would be worth their investment.

When he called back, I summarized our programs, so he would know how far we had progressed since Nyaka School opened. I encouraged him to speak with our donors. I told him my personal story about having one book in the house as a child. I even mentioned I had co-written a book about building Nyaka School.

"That's all very impressive," Jim said.

"The Nyaka Library will be just as impressive. It will serve students, teachers, and caregivers, as well as the community at large, and neighboring schools. It will become the region's principal source of access to books, news, information, and technology training."

"How much will it cost?"

"Our estimate for a five-room library is $250,000."

"I expected as much. Lynda and I are interested in funding the library, but we would like you to put in $36,000 up front."

"We can do that," I said without hesitation. The Aulds had raised $80,000 to build Kutamba School. There was money out there and I would find it. I had a grant writer now. Chris was good at what he did.

"Then we have a deal," Jim said. "As soon as you have your money raised." We shook hands.

Writing grant proposals is a time-consuming process and actually receiving a grant takes even longer. After a few months we were no closer to obtaining the library down payment. I was on the verge of breaking a promise hastily made.

One evening, I opened my *Baibuli* to *Psalms*. 33:13-22. "From heaven, the Lord looks down and sees all mankind; from His dwelling place He watches all who live on earth—He forms the hearts of all, who considers everything they do."

When I fell from a tree as a boy and a shard of wood pierced my leg, I was in the hospital for weeks. Each evening my mukaaka visited with her *Baibuli*. She would read from *Psalms*, giving me hope and helping me heal. I turned to another passage I remembered her reading.

"We wait in hope for the Lord; he is our help and our shield. In him our hearts rejoice, for we trust in his holy name. May your unfailing love be with us, Lord, even as we put our hope in you."

And so, once again, I put my trust in God. A few days later, *The Price of Stones* (re-titled *A School for My Village* in paperback) sold to Viking-Penguin Books. My share of the advance would cover Nyaka's down payment on the library.

MUHEREZA JONATHAN

My name is Muhereza Jonathan, aged 26 years old. My father is the late Arineitwe Caleb and mother the late Tindiwengi Jona. Both of them died of **HIV/AIDS**. My father was the first to die when I was around one year. This is what my grandparents tell me, and still I can't remember anything about his death. Then my mother followed when I was four years and we were left in tow, me and my sister.

I didn't know that life would be hard for me being young, and still some people had promised to take care of me for education. Life became hard for me when I and my sister started school, and the people who had promised us education were nowhere to be seen!

We fell into the care of our grandparents who were not capable of providing us with basic needs. I and my sister went to Nyakatunguru Primary School. There is a moment that I keep remembering a time when I was chased home for 500shs in school fees, I went home and sat waiting for 500shs, but all in vain.

Life became hard for me and I started regretting that our parents died when young. One year after they had died, and I was out of school with no education, people came to our home from Zeituni Seventh Day Adventist Church Kambuga. They told my grandparents to take us to Nyaka, that a school has been started for the orphans.

That was on Saturday. On Monday my grandmother took me to Nyaka. I found Mrs. Freda Byaburakyirya, who was the Head Teacher. My grandmother told her my story and I was told to go to class as the children were still very few. Immediately, I was given books and a pencil and was told to go the next day to Mr. Mureba for measurements of my uniform.

Within one week, life looked different from the situation I was in at home. I was given shoes and for the first time and I put on shoes, given a mattress and for the first time slept on a mattress, given bedsheets, blanket, toothpaste, jelly, soap, and many other items for the first time. This gave me courage and I would wake up very early and come running to school.

Something that I didn't know would come true was when I saw myself in a gown graduating when I completed my Primary-7 at Nyaka School. I went to Ishaka Adventist college where I finished my Ordinary level, and later to Bishop Comboni College Kambuga for my advanced. I went to Uganda Christian university where I have graduated with a Bachelor of Arts in Education. Am a professional teacher of History and Christian Religious Education/ Divinity and am now in the job market.

I extend my sincere thanks to the founder of Nyaka AIDS Orphans Project Dr. Jackson Kaguri for the kind heart he developed and lived with to help us orphans meet our dreams. I am now a respected person both in the community and at home, being the only person with a degree in our family. I want to thank the donors for the support they rendered me so that I can be able to meet my goal. I thank the staff of Nyaka headed by the country

Director for they have always been there for me, encouraging me, advising me, and making sure that am safe always. May the good Lord bless you abundantly.

CHAPTER 7

FAR FROM HOME

Some days I was so caught up with donors and fundraising that I did not have time to appreciate the very people I was helping—the Nyaka students. In December 2008, I was able to celebrate with our pioneer class as they graduated from Primary-7. I could not have been prouder or happier as they walked across the school yard in their purple graduation gowns. They had met their challenges head-on. So had the Nyaka Program. Not only had we had graduated our first class, but all the students except one had passed national exams and were eligible to go on to secondary school. We arranged for the student who did not pass to receive vocational training. This is what I dreamed of when we opened the school.

It was not until I returned to Michigan that reality came crashing down. Our students had a primary education, which was more than most people in the village received. They could read and write in both Rukiga and English and had a working understanding of mathematics. Maybe they could manage a shop or farm, but chances were, they would never escape the poverty of subsistence farming. For our students to become professionals and build their communities, they would need to attend secondary school and probably college.

As I stretched out on the sofa in my Michigan living room and watched Nic play a video game, I was struck by the advantages he had. If I had not received an education and come to America, my son would have been born in the village. Our lives would be focused on growing maize and beans and raising *ente* and *embuzi*. Instead, he had the whole world at his fingertips.

I wanted my Nyaka kids to have the advantages Nic enjoyed. That meant finding a way to pay for secondary boarding schools which cost about $500 annually. The Pioneer Students this year, another thirty next year, and every year after that. When Kutamba started graduating students, that would increase the total to about sixty students entering secondary school every year.

Secondary school in Uganda consists of six levels. Sixty students multiplied by six years multiplied by $500 was $180,000 per graduating class. The thought was overwhelming. God had been generous. Would He keep listening to my prayers as I asked for more and more? Would donors support the kids all the way through secondary school?

Do what is right for the kids, I told myself. *Take each year as it arrives.* We had made it this far. The money would come from somewhere.

My first choice for a secondary school was Ishaka Adventist College, located north of Nyakagyezi. It was ideal because the campus is on the hospital grounds of Ishaka Adventist Hospital and walled off from the main city. Nyaka students had never lived in a big city. I did not want them wandering around and getting into trouble. Also, my sister, Christine, works at Ishaka Primary School. She would be available to mentor.

Thanks again to generous donors, we were able to send the Pioneer class to their first year of secondary school. Most were accepted at Ishaka Adventist College. The others went to St. Gerard's Catholic School. By the next year, we had 47 students in secondary schools.

Some adapted quickly. Byamugisha Ivan took first place on his national exams for his Senior-1 class. For those who had difficulty with homesickness and academic issues at Ishaka, Christine stepped in to help.

Still, I was not happy with complaints that surfaced. Students at Ishaka struggled with outbreaks of respiratory and gastrointestinal illnesses. Most teachers did not teach in English, causing some students to begin losing what they had learned at Nyaka. If they were going on to college, they needed a firm grasp of English.

Other problems arose. Students were bullied because they were AIDS orphans. One was caught stealing food from the dorm, another disciplined for fighting at school. One of our smartest students dropped out.

I suggested to the board that we build our own secondary school, but they felt we were not ready. Unlike a primary school, which can be a simple building with seven classrooms and a kitchen, a secondary school must include dorms and labs for advanced classes. Then there were higher teachers' salaries, additional staff, and supplies. It was more money than we could hope to raise. Students would have to adapt.

I gave in to the board's logic, but it bothered me that our students were not getting the care and guidance they needed. They needed mentors, especially as they entered their teen years. Christine was doing the best she could at Ishaka, but she already had too many students to look out for.

One evening as I sat alone at my desk, I thought of how Freda had made herself available to me at any time of the day or night. What would I have done if she had not been there when my mother left? What if I had run away and not finished school?

I called Christine.

"Twesi," she said. "How are you?"

We spoke of family for a time before she told me she had some bad news.

"Ankunda Bruno is in trouble."

"What happened?"

"The students were angry they were not receiving enough food. They went on strike."

I remembered when I was Food Prefect at Kinkizi Boarding School. Probably to save money, the school served us undercooked *posho* and old beans polluted with weevil eggs and larva. A riot broke out under my watch and damage was done to the school. I was suspended. So worried was I that Taata would beat me, I did not go home, but stayed at a friend's house and found another family member to help me get reinstated.

"How long is his suspension?"

"It is worse than a suspension," Christine said.

My heart sank. "Did they expel him?"

"No, he is in jail. There was a riot and he was one of the students who threatened to burn down the school."

"God help him," I said. "Bruno has suffered enough."

Bruno's father was a well-to-do farmer with enough land to support a field of banana trees, several crops, cattle and goats, and a brick house near a natural spring. When he died in 1998, as did Bruno's mother, grandfather and aunt within the next couple of years, Bruno and his two older brothers were left to care for the property on their own. An uncle took advantage of the situation, claimed some of the land as his own, and moved Bruno's oldest brother to a neighboring town to work in his shop.

Then Bruno's middle brother had to leave to tend to their frail great-grandmother. Bruno ended up alone with just a part-time porter to watch over their inheritance—three *embuzi* and one ente.

Nyaka gave him all the support and encouragement we could. Part of that support consists of teaching our students to speak up for themselves and air grievances. Maybe Bruno was too assertive for his own good.

"I am sure he did not intend to burn the place down," I said.

"He was one of the leaders. The police are taking this very seriously."

"I wish the school had contacted us directly." We had had bad dealings with the police before. "They have not beaten him, have they?"

"No," Christine said. "I will try to get him out and speak with the headmaster."

"Thank you, Christine. You are a blessing to these kids."

Bruno spent a week in jail. Even before we had resolved this situation, another cropped up.

"Shilah has been expelled from St. Gerard's," Christine informed me. As a Catholic school, St. Gerard's had rules that our students were not familiar with.

"What is the problem?" I asked. Maybe it was just a misunderstanding.

"Shilah got an abortion."

I could not believe what I was hearing. Had we not been teaching them about HIV/AIDS for the last seven years? Shilah knew about abstaining from sex and using condoms.

Abortion is generally illegal in Uganda, punishable by up to 14 years in prison. Shilah certainly did not have money for a safe medical procedure. Her only choice would have been a traditional healer supplying her with herbs to induce abortion. Other more drastic measures might have been used. I shivered at the thought. She was lucky to have survived.

"Did an older man take advantage of her?" I said. Rukungiri is a big city compared to Nyakagyezi.

"No, she had a boyfriend."

"What can we do for her? She needs to finish school." We discussed options and Shirah was eventually able to return to her schooling.

By the end of the Pioneer class' third year of secondary school, we had eight pregnant girls, three students suspended, and one accused of stealing food to sell in the dorm.

I felt guilty. When I was in the village, I treated the students as my own children, but I could not be there now. Christine tried to be a mother-figure to the ones at Ishaka, but she did not have enough hours in the day to give them all quality time. It was becoming obvious that a distant secondary school was more of a change than our students were able to manage. Not only was I failing them, the Nyaka program was failing them. We needed a secondary school.

It no longer mattered what the board advised. These were my kids and I was going to make sure they were cared for.

TUKAMUSHABA ANNITAH

Tukamushaba Annitah went through Primary-7 at Nyaka Primary School. She attended Ishaka Adventist Secondary School in Bushenyi but dropped out in her second year.

She got married and is now a single mother of two children (6 years and 1.5 years). The father of the older child died in an accident and the boy is staying with his grandfather. Annitah owns a small business selling *matooke* and charcoal. She lives in Kampala.

CHAPTER 8

TAKING A STAND

While we were succeeding in our efforts to educate a handful of the estimated 5,000 orphans in Kanungu District, I was forever reminded that so many more needed our help. When we first opened Nyaka School, we had more than 100 children apply for fifty-six openings. Since then we have had even more applicants for our limited slots. To make the difficult selection less painful, we give priority to double orphans who lost both parents. We have hard and fast rules, but on rare occasions, rules can be broken.

Allan Akamumpa was one student who benefited from such a decision. Allan was a thin eight-year-old with hands frozen in grasping positions, arms locked at the wrist. His legs below the knees were like sticks and his feet twisted to the side so that he could not stand. No one knew what had afflicted him since birth. There was no doctor in the village to diagnose him, and no money to pay for treatment.

It is common in Uganda for people to shun those with deformities and physical disabilities. People often believe these afflictions are caused by a curse from God and associating with a disabled person will bring the curse upon themselves. It was surprising that Allan's mother allowed him to be seen in public.

When Nyaka School opened, Allan was determined to attend. He crawled to the school on his fists and knees along a dirt road littered with stones and ente dung. What would take an average person five minutes to walk, took Allan hours to navigate. After witnessing this arduous journey each day for two weeks Freda Byaburakiirya, who had come out of retirement as a volunteer to help get Nyaka School up and running, brought up the issue during one of our phone conversations.

"We have a problem with Allan Akamumpa. He crawls to school each day. By the time he reaches us, classes are finished. I feel so bad. What should we do?" Freda had taught thousands of children over the years and Allan held a special place in her heart.

"Allan is not an AIDS orphan," I said. His parents were poor and had three other children. His mother did chores for other people to make money. "It is not fair to the other children to take him in."

"He is sort of an orphan," Freda said, "given his situation." Her heart is big enough to adopt every orphan in the village. If she had her way, we would take all the applicants.

"If we make one exception, there will be others."

"Allan suffers more than the rest," she said. "You know that, Twesi."

I remembered when my mother, sick of my father's abusive behavior, walked out on him. She traveled across the country to stay with my uncle, leaving me and two sisters at home, motherless. Freda had stepped in to nurture me as a second mother. If not for her, I might have turned into an angry young man with no goals. It did not matter to her if a child was her own. All children were her children.

"Allan needs to attend school," she said.

"I suppose you will not take no for an answer." She did not have to answer the question. When Freda sets her mind to something, it gets done. A few weeks later, Allan was accepted into the Primary-1 class.

Getting Allan to class was another matter. His father volunteered to bring him, but their only vehicle was an old bicycle. Every morning, he lifted Allan onto the seat, making sure his legs were clear of the front tire. Only one of Allan's hands was dexterous enough to wrap around a handlebar. Balancing Allan on the seat, his father pushed the bike up a rugged incline to the school gates. From there, the grassy lawn was another uphill push.

Nothing in the village is designed to be handicapped-accessible and Nyaka School is no exception. There is a large a step up to reach a cement platform along the building's outer edge and additional steps into each classroom. The bike got Allan to the front of the school. He had to crawl from there.

Maybe because they were orphans, the students understood instinctively that Allan needed extra attention. They soon took it upon themselves to carry him between classrooms, to the latrine, to the grassy yard for lunch break. Someone would get his plate of food and help him eat. His hand would not open, so another student inserted a pencil between his frozen fingers.

It took time and patience, but Allan learned to write. Before long, his classmates were not only helping at school, but pushing his bike back and forth to school each day.

Getting medical help for Allan was a topic of discussion among board members and teachers for many months. There was only a small rural hospital in nearby Kambuga. With one doctor and a handful of nurses, they were not equipped to take care of a paralyzed boy with no diagnosis and an unknown future. Help might be available in Kampala, but that was an eight-hour journey from the village. We had no money to pay for transportation, housing, and medical care. We did not even know if anything could be done to help him.

Not long after we opened Kutamba School, one of our board members contacted a pediatrician in Kampala. Dr. Sebuliba agreed to see Allan. As it happened, Ira Zinman, a Rotarian from Bloomington, was making a film about the school and was in Uganda at the time. Under Ira's direction, his cinematographer, Kirsten Scully, accompanied Allan and his father to Kampala's Mulago Teaching Hospital.

"His prognosis would be better if he'd come to us at a much earlier age," Dr. Sebuliba told them. He carefully manipulated Allan's legs, feet, and hands. They were rigid but showed some potential for movement. "The ligaments and tendons are stiff from lack of use. The muscles are underdeveloped. If he was four or five, I would have more hope for him."

"Is it possible for him to stand if he gets help?" Kirsten asked.

"The boy probably only has one growth spurt left," Dr. Sebuliba said. "With surgery and physical therapy, there's a possibility he can be self-sufficient. It will take several months, maybe a year."

Allan's father could not move to Kampala for the many months it would take Allan to undergo surgery and rehabilitation. Kirsten contacted Ira with the news, and Ira suggested Allan come to the United States for treatment. He contacted Naomi Corera, director of Children Waiting Everywhere, an Ann Arbor foundation that operates in Uganda. She convinced doctors at The University of

Michigan Hospital to consider taking Allan's case.

The University of Michigan operates a hospital in Fort Portal, Uganda, a tourist town and the seat of Kabarole District and the Toro Kingdom. It is scenically located between Lake Edward and Lake Albert just east of the Rwenzori National Park and the Mountains of the Moon. People travel from all parts of the globe to see the wildlife, crater lakes, and natural beauty of the area.

Virika Hospital's mission is to serve the poor. It is a non-profit community hospital supported by the Stephen M. Ross School of Business at the University of Michigan, the U-M Medical School, and the William Davidson Institute at the University of Michigan. In April 2008, Allan's father accompanied him on the four-hour journey to visit doctors there. After an extensive exam, they sent a report to U-M Medical School indicating that he could be helped. He was accepted for treatment in November of that year.

That was the first hurdle. The next problem was finding money to get Allan to the United States and a place to stay. Once again Rotarians, along with Nyaka supporters Whitney Gates and Harriet Lewis, stepped up to raise the necessary funding. Naomi Corera proposed Ken and Patti Cousino as a host family for Allan. As parents of 11 children, they had plenty of experience. With only their youngest son still at home, they also had room. Ken and Patti were happy to help.

Another hurdle jumped. Now we needed visas. Once again, Allan's father travelled to Kampala where the US Embassy helped him fill out paperwork. He waited weeks for a response.

"We're sorry," the embassy woman said. "We can't grant you and your son a visa. You lack the financial and family ties to ensure that you will return to Uganda."

I was not surprised. I had invited my sisters to visit Michigan several times. Each time they tried to get a visa they were refused. The United States did not want poor Ugandans sneaking into the country. If there was any indication a person might try to stay, the answer was "No. No. No."

Ira was not happy when I called him with the news.

"I can't believe this," he said. "We've got airline tickets paid for, we have a host family, we have doctors willing to help him for free, and he can't get a visa?"

"This happens all the time," I said. "I know very few who receive a visa on their first try. He will apply again."

"We don't have much time," Ira said. "Allan is almost too old for treatment as it is. If we delay a year or two, they might not be able to help him at all."

"I know," I said.

The third time the visa application was rejected, I worried. We contacted the doctors at the Fort Portal Hospital and asked if anyone there could help. They understood the urgency of the situation.

Eventually, we were contacted by Father George Ahairwe of the Fort Portal Diocese. He had a visa and volunteered to be Allan's guardian while he visited America. We were all relieved.

Allan arrived in Ann Arbor late in November. Not only did he have to adjust to living with a new family, but also his first winter. Ken and Patti met him at the airport with a heavy parka, gloves, and warm clothing. When Patti asked him to open his suitcase at their house, she was amazed.

"There was only millet flour, ground nuts and grasshoppers. He thought he was bringing us a delicacy, but those grasshoppers were scary." Culture shock works both ways.

It was snowing when Allan arrived at the hospital. He was

evaluated by Dr. Edward Wojtys and physical therapist, Steven Blum. They assessed Allan's flexibility and diagnosed him with a form of cerebral palsy. They agreed to try surgery but could not guarantee success.

"Normally, we would address a condition like this when a child is two to five years old, maybe up to eight." Allan was almost 13.

By March 2009, Allan was using his legs to propel an adult-sized tricycle along the halls. He bustled with energy. A few months later, he was using a walker to take his first steps. On his fourteenth birthday, Allan stood up on his own for the first time ever.

When his visa expired the following November, Allan left for Uganda in a wheelchair. Ken Cousino and Ryan Tritch travelled with him to Nyaka. The village celebrated his return as Ken pushed him up the hill in his wheelchair. When Allan raised himself to a standing position, the kids cheered and broke into song:

> *"Bright shining, shining.*
> *Time is going, and we must work hard for peace and*
> *   prosperity.*
> *We are the instruments of change in Uganda and we*
> *   will put it among the Nations raising."*

From the school, they paraded to Freda's house with Allan leading the way. Freda's face lit when she saw him in his wheelchair.

"You. You. You," she said. "My Allan." She kissed the top of his head and hugged him.

Allan stood and Freda nearly fainted.

"Thanks be to God," she shouted. "God is great. Halleluiah."

To increase muscle strength, Allan needed a smooth surface to practice with his special walker. There was no level area at his house which sat near the rutted road. But God works in mysterious ways. The unfinished basketball court became the perfect surface for physical therapy.

Allan completed his primary education. Because he still has limited mobility, Nyaka paid for him to receive computer training in Kampala. Today he lives in the village, uses a walker, and works part-time for the headmaster at Nyaka School.

SHIRAH OWOMUGISHA

I am Shirah Owomugisha, twenty-three years old, from the strikingly beautiful country of Uganda, from a small village in the southern part of Uganda called Kambuga, Nyakagyezi. I reflect a varied personality including ambition and the qualities of generosity and thoughtfulness. I am also a well determined and vigorous individual, yet pleasantly calm. I encourage fighting for what you desire and believe in and doing it through God because nothing great comes easy and with God everything is possible.

I attended my primary education at Nyaka Primary School in kanungu district and later went to Ishaka Adventist College for my S1-S4 in Bushenyi district, where I later had my High school at San Giovani School-Makiiro in Kanungu.

I am now a full-time student at Vancouver Island University, and I stay in Canada, Vancouver BC, motivated by my love for learning and succeeding as I strive to become an outstanding and successful woman. With the definitive goal of studying Management at VIU, I would love to have my own Management consulting company. I am currently completing the Bachelor's degree Program in Business Management.

Apart from the above, I have kept a keen interest in volunteering and enjoy reading, gym and taking dancing classes. The Bible is the book I spend most time reading, but science fictional Stories are more appealing to my imagination. I don't have a favorite writer; however, I have had the pleasure to bask in the creativity of authors like Dan Brown, who is known for his famous *Da Vinci Code*, and Jules Verne, author of *Journey to the Centre of the Earth.*

CHAPTER 9

HOW OUR GARDEN GREW

While Allan was in Michigan, Nyaka prepared to host a visitor from Colorado. Carol Auld and her team had put their Aspen Nyaka volunteers to work finding someone to develop a gardening program to help us efficiently produce food for our students and their *mukaakas*.

Eden Vardy was a young entrepreneur who moved to Aspen from Israel. In 2008, he and his wife founded Aspen **TREE**, their goal being to give kids the necessary tools and inspiration to grow food in an environmentally friendly way. Their programming includes interactions with farm animals, gardening, nature discovery, traditional arts and crafts, and solar cooking.

When Nyaka Primary School opened as a two-room school, I wanted meals to be part of a comprehensive program, but we had no money. Later students were served a breakfast of hot milk or porridge and a roll or pastry. Now that Kutamba was open, we had 244 students to feed. We were also feeding lunch to children in Primary-3 through -6.

We initially hired a local caterer, but the expense was becoming a problem. What we really needed was a way to grow our own produce. We decided to transform a portion of Nyaka School's property into a garden. Eden was just the person to help us.

He arrived in the village in January 2009, a thin young man with curly black hair and a wide smile. By this time, we had built a guest house for visitors used to modern luxuries like running water, toilets, and showers. Even so, Eden experienced the culture shock that many of our visitors must deal with. It can be overwhelming to be the only *muzungu* for miles around, all eyes watching, and children following because they are curious about your white skin.

Eden's discomfort was compounded by concern that the villagers he passed along the way to Nyaka were already practicing permaculture techniques. What would he teach them that they did not already know? Once he understood the scope of our need, his misgivings subsided. Our site was a blank slate and our students eager to learn what he would do with it. Discomfort transformed into professional excitement. He was ready to get to work.

By the end of the month, Eden had teamed up with Agaba Innocent and Steven Kafunzi to construct the Nyaka Demonstration Garden. There were no tractors with plows in the village. It was all done manually using shovels and hoes with foot-wide blades. Trees were cut down and sawed by hand to provide boards as needed. Every process was labor intensive.

Our permaculture system includes goats and chickens. Eden designed an elevated goat pen with slits in the floor to allow collection of manure as a primary fertilizer. The goat house is also equipped with a water harvesting tank to provide clean drinking water for the animals. A chicken coop supplies eggs and generates fertilizer while its inhabitants prepare the soil through scratching.

The vegetable garden is laid out in a mandala keyhole design.

This pattern creates more edges to increase diversity and productivity. The basic idea is that it provides easy access with a minimal path-to-bed ratio. Horseshoe-shaped beds are sized to allow a person to easily reach the entire area while standing in the keyhole.

The Primary-7 class in their purple Nyaka uniforms began to mulch the garden on February 9th. Mulch was composed of layers of banana leaves, manure, coffee husks, dry grass and food scraps. The students quickly turned this chore from work into fun, singing and competing.

When the garden was complete, every class received a plot to maintain. Gardening was scheduled into Nyaka class time. *Mukaakas* were also given a garden bed. Another section of the garden became the food forest.

The Primary-2 class planted trees on February 10th, the Tu'B Shvat or Hebrew birthday of trees. Eden, inspired by the kids' excitement, assigned a tree to each student.

"This will be your very own tree until you graduate from Nyaka School," he said.

The food forest contains banana and papaya trees with an understory of coffee trees. The ground beneath sustains groundnuts and pumpkins. Avocado, mango, and jackfruit trees are planted around the perimeter.

Of course, everything in the village happens on Uganda time. This was difficult for Eden to adapt to, especially since he had a limited timeframe to complete the project. Often, workers would stop to chat with him.

"Are there poor people in America?" Agaba asked on one such occasion.

"Of course," Eden said. "But it's different. In some ways, the poor in America are worse off than here. They often live on the streets and don't have access to natural food sources."

"Wow," Agaba said. "How can it be that they do not know people who grow food to share or work for?"

It was difficult for Eden to explain that most Americans do not grow their own food. Even people with property in the suburbs buy food at grocery stores. He tried his best, but Agaba still seemed confused after the explanation.

"I have another question for you. Why is it that so many groups come from America to help Ugandans and Africa as a whole? Why do they not help the poor Americans?"

That question was even more difficult. Agaba could not grasp the idea of a social welfare system that is supposed to take care of the needy. He also did not understand the resentment many feel when it comes to using their tax dollars to care for the poor. This complex situation of taxes, expectations, and work ethic was entirely foreign. If you are poor in the United States people think you are unwilling to work. In Uganda, if you are poor, people know you cannot work.

Eden tried a new approach. "People in foreign lands living on a dollar a day appear needier because it costs more to live there. An American dollar can buy so much more here."

"Ah," Agaba said. "That makes sense. Spend your money where it will get the most and you will have more money left to spend." He tapped his forehead and went back to work.

Everything was planted by March 1st. The garden was soon bulging with banana trees, corn, cabbages, and beans. We hired Agaba to manage it and educate the local community about the processes and principles involved. Students and their guardians attended weekly classes on integrated pest management, how to cultivate flowering plants to attract beneficial insects, growing legumes and grasses together, composting and mulching, transplanting, and many other techniques.

The garden program helped surrounding farmers and supplied students with extra food to take home. It was so successful that we began a garden program at Kutamba later in the year. But, on that hill, the gardens were not large enough to supply students with two meals a day.

If we were going to grow enough food for everyone, we needed more land and that would take money. Once again, the Aulds stepped in to help. Two of their friends, Elaine Grossman and Tory Dietel, raised enough to buy ten acres one mile from Nyaka.

It took 700 labor-days to get Desire Farm running: 200 for stumping and clearing, 400 for tilling, and 100 for planting. A local manager was hired and grandmothers, along with day laborers, took on the job of caring for the land and its bounty. They are paid 2,500 Ugandan Shillings per day (about $1.30), which is considered a good wage.

Our first planting season was over the 2009-10 winter. We sowed all ten acres and harvested 880 pounds of dried beans and sweet potatoes and 2.5 tons of maize. We produced enough extra to pay for teacher and staff training workshops in 2010.

One of our board members from Michigan donated money to purchase our first milk cow. We named her Genesis. Cows and goats are considered assets in the village.

Each time Nic visits, he receives cows, goats, or sheep as gifts. Any young man in Uganda would be envious of his large herd, and his business insight. It did not take Nic long to learn the value of his animals. After pestering me unsuccessfully to get a cellphone, he approached me with a new idea.

"Dad," he announced. "I know how to pay for a phone."

I frowned. "By getting a job?" Even though Nic had visited the village many times, he did not appreciate the amount of physical labor someone his age would be doing there. A boy there would tend animals before and after school, fetch water and wood for cooking, and do his studying in semi-darkness under lamp light. There was no time for video games or cellphones.

"Not a job," he said. "I have more cows than I need. I'll sell one to pay for the phone."

I had to admit it was a clever idea. The cows were his property to do with as he wanted. "Okay, we will have your *shwenkuru* sell one for you."

As I dealt with a growing boy who had inherited some of his grandfather's shrewdness, the farm became a critical part of our Vocational Training Program for graduates of Nyaka and Kutamba who would not attend secondary school. The farm is a hotbed of innovation and agricultural learning. For a fee, farmers come to learn seeding, transplanting, grafting, fertilizing, and weeding techniques. They also gain access to valuable information about how to farm with improved hybrid seeds, ordinarily a risky initiative for the uneducated. We cultivate maize, kale, okra, onions, carrots, cabbage, beans, and bananas. We have cows and chickens to provide milk and eggs. Students are taught the same forward-looking skills as established farmers who pay to attend.

Desire Farm is a continuing success that helps to prove the value of a holistic approach.

DESIRE FARM

Desire Farm is ten acres and grows crops, including maize, kale, okra, onions, carrots, cabbage, beans, and bananas. Cows and chickens provide milk and eggs. Students learn seeding, transplanting, grafting, fertilizing, and weeding techniques. For a small fee, local farmers can also come to Desire Farm and learn farming techniques.

Genesis with her calf at Desire Farm.

CHAPTER 10

CRACKS IN THE FOUNDATION

While the garden was being constructed, I returned my focus to the library project. There was nowhere to build it near Nyaka School. I tried to negotiate with several neighbors, but very few owned enough property to hold a library. Freda and Patrick Byaburakirya possessed enough acres, but the family could not agree on selling a portion of it.

I mulled over the situation. I wanted the library as close to Nyaka School as possible, but the only land I could find was a twenty-minute walk down the dirt road to Kambuga. My maternal uncle had sold us land to build Desire Farm and he had more unused acreage adjacent to that location. It was not entirely flat but spread across the crest of a hill. With Tory Dietel's help we purchased that plot.

Matt, the Kutamba architect, volunteered to do the design. It was to be a U-shaped building containing everything I had asked from Jim and Lynda Martin. Things went smoothly until I learned we were expected get three bids.

This is how things are done in the United States and Canada, especially for government jobs. Several companies present sealed bids and the lowest competitive offer receives the contract. It makes logical sense. A company can get a job done for the least amount of money.

I worried. Over the years, in the many personal and business projects I have completed, I have had to deal with stolen materials and unscrupulous business owners. I know which contractors are reliable.

We had to advertise this project in national newspapers and ended up with a Kampala City company. I could not be on-site during construction, and my father lived too far away to keep an eye on the workers. I had to have faith they would do a good job.

When I arrived in Uganda that year, I wanted to focus on the library, but many people were more interested in my marital status. Taata had been unusually quiet about the divorce, but I am sure he felt vindicated that my marriage to an American had not worked worked out.

"I have a woman you should meet," my good friend Emma Mugisha said. She is a prominent Kampala banker and her friends are well-educated and sincere. The woman she introduced me to was very nice but seemed more interested in marriage than getting to know me.

It was worse in the village. When I was a young man with no money, local women saw me as a friend, maybe even as a good-looking man, but they were never in a hurry to get married. Now my reputation arrived before I did. I was considered a rich American, the Nyaka Director, and the best catch in town. It did not matter if I had bad teeth, was abusive, or what religious beliefs I held.

I found myself watching every word I said around eligible

women. What I saw as a handshake and a greeting they might interpret as interest in dating them. I only wanted to be friendly and they were making wedding plans.

Large events were particularly stressful. I was very happy to see Nyaka board members Msunguzi Wilfred, Ndyabahika Stanley, and Sempa Baker at the library groundbreaking. Sam Mugisha took time away from his tour business to join us. Rob Auld came from Aspen. But hundreds of women also showed up. Everyone was excited about the new building, but there were some in the crowd who had come to look me over like a prized bull. I had spent many evenings alone in my Michigan office wishing I had a life partner, but this was not the way I wanted to find her.

After the groundbreaking, Mr. Silver Ndazororera volunteered to host an organizational meeting at his house to discuss plans for the library and how the community could participate. He was a public servant who worked as a clerk for local judges. His wife, Leonarda, was a teacher and one of the few grannies in our program who could speak English. She had gone to Toronto with Freda in 2006 to attend the Stephen Lewis Foundation Granny Event before Nyaka became part of their formal program. All five of their children had received a university education.

Mr. Silver's house was just over the hill from my parents' home, near the Catholic church and the secondary school I attended as a boy. By the time I arrived there were already fifteen people congregated in a yard bordered by trellised passion fruit vines heavy with green fruits. I spotted Mr. Silver in a black suit near the entrance to his stucco home.

"*Oreiregye Mzee,*" I said.

"*Yego. Agandi,*" he replied.

"This is more people than I expected," I said.

"Many are interested in this library. Even people who cannot read."

Sam and Stanley soon arrived. They were followed by several town and religious leaders and interested citizens. In all a crowd of about thirty men and women gathered to discuss the library.

Silver and Leonarda may have planned to meet inside their house, but the crowd was too large. Two men dragged wooden benches and chairs out outside and we gathered in the shade of a tree.

"*Mureiregye*," I said. "Thank you all for coming. Now that we have broken ground for the library building, it is important to have you all involved. Our plan includes five rooms, three children's reading rooms organized by reading level, a fourth room for a general lending library, and a fifth multipurpose room with a public-address system. Eventually we will have computers." My dream is to get a book into the hands of every child. I believe books are like toys. They should be read, played with, torn, and used in every way. Books are a gateway to so much and that gate should be opened early in life.

A woman raised her hand. "I do not understand," she said. "Is this another school? Why are there so many rooms?"

"This is not a school," I said. "It will be a place that community members like you, students, and adults can come to read and borrow books." For most in the village, the only libraries they knew were small rooms with a few shelves located in school buildings.

"I could go there?" she asked. "To find a book?"

"Yes. It will be open to everyone in the village. There will be newspapers as well as books to read."

"What about teachers?" I recognized the man asking the question as one of the teachers from the nearest government school called Zooroma. As a previous student of the public-school system, I was familiar with the plight of teachers. They were always in short supply of books and materials.

"Yes, it will be open to teachers too."

"The schools should pay a membership fee," Wilfred said. He was our financial advisor and always had good suggestions. He and Stanley had studied business at the university.

The discussion continued. We talked about the purpose of the library, ways of getting a steady supply of books and informing the public about what was available. My maternal uncle, Mpeeka, stood grandly, obviously proud of his nephew.

He set his square jaw. "Will the library be open during school holidays? When students are home during those weeks, they end up loitering around the businesses and getting in trouble with boda boda guys in town."

I had not considered that. "That is a good point. We want the library to be a place where people can read, meet, relax, and discuss ideas."

"What about a canteen?" someone suggested.

"Another good idea." Maybe, instead of different reading rooms for different ages, we could expand on the idea of the library being a community center.

We planned several meetings between teachers, board members, and community members and agreed to conduct additional sensitization meetings at churches and public gatherings. I repeatedly emphasized that this would be a community-led and community-owned library. We would eventually have computers powered by solar cells. Textbooks would be purchased. We would charge schools a small membership fee to access them.

The meeting adjourned with everyone feeling a sense of

community pride. The Kambuga-Nyakagyezi area was about to have the first lending library in western Uganda. Everyone was excited. This library would not only offer books, but help to enrich the community and improve social, spiritual, economic, and educational standards.

Construction began early in 2009. The workers looked very professional in their blue and yellow jumpsuits and my worry that there might be problems eased. This was a business from Kampala, where competition and expectations were higher than in the village. Surely, everything would go as planned.

The ground was cleared, the foundation laid, and brick walls quickly rose. The building was topped with red metal roofing on schedule. We scheduled the grand opening for April 26th, 2010.

I envisioned The Blue Lupin Library as a wonderful community resource that could be used by church groups and service organizations. Secondary students could use it to study and hang out with classmates at the canteen. Computers would allow students to learn Microsoft Excel, Word, and eventually how to use the internet to better prepare them for university. The library would also be a resource for literate residents who wanted to read a newspaper.

Early one morning after I dropped Nic at school, a call came from the building committee manager.

"*Agandi*," he said.

"*Nigye.*" I leaned over the kitchen sink and glanced out the back window at the snow-covered yard, wishing I was with him where the daytime temperature was in the 80s.

It did not take long for the bad news to come out. "The floor of the library is cracking."

"What?"

"The cement floor. It is cracking in several places. We think the contractors failed to put a moisture barrier between the cement and the earth."

"Oh, no." I should have stood my ground and used contractors I knew, but it was too late now. "They will have to replace the floors. We will not accept poor workmanship."

"That is what I told them, but they said they cannot replace the cement."

"Why not?" I paced the length of the kitchen. "They guaranteed their work. They should have insurance that will cover the mistake. Tell them to dig up the floors and pour new cement."

There was a pause.

"Hello?"

"That is another problem. They are not insured."

"God, help us," I said. We had just spent $150,000 on a building and the floors were cracking before it even opened.

"They said the building is sound, the footers are good. It is only the floors. They can try to patch them."

I took a deep breath, trying to calm my anger. "Okay. Have them do that. There is not much else we can accomplish now." The library would open in April, cracked floors or not.

Hundreds of people came to the grand opening. The shelves held only a few books and some rooms were empty, but people were impressed with the building. If they noticed the patched floors, no one said a thing. I reminded myself that most people in the area had only dirt floors. It was the availability of books and other reading materials that was important. If we created literacy and improved reading skills in the community, the project would be a success.

BLUE LUPIN LIBRARY

Construction of the Blue Lupin Community Library started in
2009.

The library was completed in 2010 and now provides access to newspapers, literature, computers, solar powered Wi-Fi, and a safe place for thousands of students and community members. The library also has office space for Nyaka Staff members and a meeting room for trainings.

CHAPTER 11

MUMMY DRAYTON

It seems that sometimes God ignores my prayers. At other times, He listens too closely. The entire 2009 year was one of those times. Nyaka graduates settled into their secondary schools, the library was under construction and we had everything ready to open Desire Farm. If someone had told me that we would be starting yet another project I would not have believed them.

When we first opened Nyaka School, we found that students in poor health missed school and when they did attend, they did not do well in their studies. There was only one physician at the hospital in Kambuga to care for 250,000 people. Wait times were long. The hospital was far and paying for transportation and medical costs was more than we could afford.

Although I wished we could build a clinic, we hired a part-time nurse to treat students at the school for common ailments such as malaria, ringworm, coughs, and colds. That might have been enough, but we did not plan for people dropping by to seek medical care. Our nurse, Gloria, delivered two babies in the school compound that first year.

I suggested building a clinic to the board several times, but each time they reminded me that we were a school. We could not be everything to everyone. I suggested we at least employ a full-time nurse. In 2007, they gave in to that demand and promoted Gloria to full time. Her job now was not only to treat the kids at school, but to make home visits.

Traveling to student homes was an all-day affair. Typically, it involved walking a trail down the steep Enengo to visit a *mukaaka* who might care for several grandchildren. Many houses were in poor condition. Mud-daub huts with no windows and banana-leaf roofs often leaked. If the family was lucky, they had a bed and a blanket to keep them warm at night. Often, children slept on the dirt floor. If the house did not have a deep pit latrine, its occupants would relieve themselves in the surrounding area where they grew banana trees or other produce. For *mukaakas* without a separate kitchen building, cooking was done outside over a fire or on an inside fire pit that exposed the entire family to smoke. This could lead to respiratory problems. Children were constantly at risk of disease in such conditions.

Gloria's first goal was to teach the family correct sanitation and hygiene. By this time, we had installed our first gravity-fed water system. Families close to the school now had a source of clean water, but many did not understand that using a dirty jerrycan defeated the purpose. They had to be educated.

We had been giving mosquito nets to families for a couple years, but adults often kept the nets for themselves, leaving the children vulnerable. Malaria remained a problem and many students required treatment. We were also testing students for HIV. Adults will not invest resources in a child they think will die of AIDS, and these tests reassure relatives the child is not infected.

They also enable us to identify the few children who do need anti-retroviral medications.

Nurse Gloria was on the front line for all of this and more. Meeting with *mukaakas* in their 70s and 80s brought its own challenges. If a *mukaaka* was ill or in pain because of a bad tooth, the student would miss school to stay home and help her. We needed to aid the entire family if Nyaka was to succeed.

Gloria treated *mukaakas* suffering from sore bones, stomach ulcers and high blood pressure as best she could. Aspirin, anti-fungal cream, and bandages helped, but she was soon overwhelmed. In 2008, we hired a second full-time nurse. Between the two of them, they treated more than 450 students and about 300 guardians that year. We still had no dental care.

That same year, we were blessed to have a group of nurses visit from the United States. These middle-aged angels came armed with both experience and medications. We built bunk beds in the guest house to accommodate them while they worked at Kambuga Hospital. From the kindness in their hearts, they and the hospital doctor offered a free Saturday clinic at the school.

No one anticipated the hundreds of people who showed up that day. A school room had been set aside as an exam room, but the nurses ended up creating satellite stations throughout the school yard. Even with that, people waited for hours. The nurses treated things as simple as ringworm to serious open wounds. They even did HIV testing.

By the end of the day, the demand for free medical care in the area was obvious. We needed a real clinic. I would have to put on my stubborn suit and convince the board of directors. Then, of course, I would have to find the money.

One board member, Nancy Colier, took my pleas seriously. A

psychotherapist and ordained interfaith minister by training, she teaches mindfulness, is a relationship coach, and writes. Her focus on eastern spirituality gives her a holistic, grounded approach that has been very important for the school and our organization.

Nancy recommended that Reverend Ingrid Scott call the office. Ingrid ran a manufacturing company in England for thirty years before starting the CBD Interfaith Ministry. Her second business was an inspirational mail-order company. She also runs Angelic Motivational Workshops, a ministry, and the CBD Charitable Trust.

Ingrid called the day after Thanksgiving 2009. "I'm not doing any Black Friday shopping for myself," she said in her British accent. "I want you and me to go shopping."

"Here in Michigan?"

Ingrid laughed. "I have a charitable trust and I'm most interested in education for girls and enterprises for women. What does Nyaka need?"

I was stunned. I spend half my time trying to locate donors and the other half writing grant proposals and giving talks to promote Nyaka. I had never had someone call out of the blue and ask what I needed.

My mind raced. She liked education. With Nyaka and Kutamba schools graduating students, it was becoming clear what we needed.

"A secondary school," I said.

"That's out of my price range, I should think."

Of course, it was. What was I thinking? I hoped she did not think I was selfish. I was asking for the most expensive project Nyaka would ever consider.

"A clinic," I said. "We have two nurses on staff to care for students and their families, but there is a great need for medical care in the district." I told her about the babies that had been delivered, and how our visiting nurses had to turn people away. "We also need a dentist. We give the children toothbrushes, but there is no one to check their teeth. Many of our grandmothers have serious dental and eye problems."

"Do you have programs for pregnant women?"

"We need everything," I said. "Classes for pregnant women, childbirth training, birth control, childcare training after the baby is born."

"All righty," she said. "You're depressing me now."

"Sorry. Maybe you would be interested in a smaller project. We are..."

"No," she said. "I'm interested in the clinic. Find out how much it will cost and call me back."

Because of the time difference between Uganda and Michigan, I had to wait several hours before I could speak to Sempa Baker, our accountant in Kampala.

"There is a woman from London who is interested in donating toward the cost of the clinic," I said.

"I thought we were not building a clinic. Isn't that what the board decided?"

"It is not a priority," I said. "But this woman is offering to help. I cannot say no."

"A clinic will cost at least $60,000," Sempa said. "Who is this woman? Is she paying for all of it?"

"She is a minister," I said. "She used to have a business and now runs a charity." I did not know much about her but imagined what I thought of as a "typical" British woman: white, affluent, dressed in a conservative blue business suit. "I told her I would call her back with a price estimate."

"Tell her $60,000," Sempa said. "I can get a more exact figure if she remains interested."

I called Ingrid the next day.

"My mum passed away not long ago and left me an inheritance," she said. "I will admit I didn't get on with Mum very well. I told my brother he could have the money, but he didn't want it. So, it needs to go to a good cause."

"Would you like the donation in her name?"

"No," she said. "On second thought, is it possible to name the clinic?"

"Of course, but Nyaka must be included too."

"We called my mother Mummy Drayton."

"We can call it the Nyaka Mummy Drayton Clinic," I said.

"I like that. I'll get the money to you as soon as possible. Send me wiring instructions."

Ingrid and I spoke several more times. On my next trip to Uganda, I had a layover at Heathrow Airport, where she agreed to meet me. I waited near the airport pick-up for her to arrive. Plenty of women walked by—a tall one with red hair in a black business suit, a plump one in a flowered dress, one with a silver cell phone pressed to her ear, another with an enormous green handbag. None gave me so much as a nod of recognition.

I was not paying attention to the middle-aged, light-skinned black woman. "Twesigye Jackson Kaguri?" she said, extending her hand.

"Ingrid Scott?" She was not *muzungu*. I have to admit, I was delighted. Our girls need to see and know that women who look like them can impact the world. I shook Ingrid's hand, hoping she did not notice my initial confusion.

Not long after I met Ingrid, I received another surprising call.

"My name is John Brewster," the man said. "I'm a dentist here in Okemos."

He explained that the American Dental Association maintains lists of organizations that send dentists to underprivileged regions where people cannot receive dental care. He had traveled with Medical Teams International to Cambodia, the Amazon region, and to a clinic in Bosco Ekya, northern Uganda.

"I saw your book in the bookstore," he said. "I couldn't believe you live right here in town."

As it happens, we live a little over a mile from each other. He is also a Rotarian, but a member of the Okemos Rotary, while I attend meetings at the East Lansing chapter. He asked if we needed a dentist to visit the village.

"Yes," I said. "The village has never had a dentist. We are building a medical clinic now."

"I would like to offer my services," he said.

"Certainly. If there is any equipment you need, let me know. We will include it in our building plan."

God answered my prayers before I even said them. And in 2013, Dr. Leah Greenspan Hodor, a neonatologist who founded Vital Health Africa, brought her expertise to Nyaka. We soon invited her to become our Medical Advisor. We are truly blessed.

MUMMY DRAYTON CLINIC

The Mummy Drayton School Clinic was completed in 2011. It was built to provide basic healthcare services, **HIV/AIDS** testing, immunizations, and medicine to our students, grandmothers, and community members. Dental, chiropractic, and other health services are sometimes also conducted by volunteers who are visiting Nyaka.

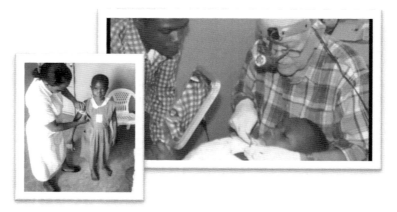

CHAPTER 12

IT TAKES A SINGLE MAN

I thought 2009 was a busy year. Little did I know it was only the beginning of my ride along the rapids of life. In 2010, the book I was working on with Susan Linville was published.

Susan and I met in 2003, a few days after an article about Nyaka School appeared in the *Bloomington Herald Times*. She called, explaining that she had watched an episode of Oprah that took place in South Africa. Oprah talked about the AIDs crisis and brought gifts for hundreds of orphaned children.

"I wanted to do something," she said, "so I bought 30 backpacks. They're purple to match the Nyaka uniforms. And I've included pencils and other school supplies and would like to donate them."

We made plans to meet at the psychology building of Indiana University where her office was located. I arrived in the main lobby with Nic and was met by a middle-aged woman with curly brown hair, a large cardboard box balanced atop her arms. In those days, any contribution was welcome, though money would have been preferred. It was expensive to ship her donation to the school, so I had to transport the backpacks to Uganda in my luggage.

I invited Susan to a fundraising dinner. About twenty people showed up and encouraged her to become part of Indiana Friends of Nyaka. This small group took on the task of sponsoring yearly banquets that, over time, raised thousands of dollars for the program. At one of these meetings I first mentioned the idea of writing a book about my life and building the school.

"I can write," Susan said. "I'll help you with the book. If we sell it to a publisher, we'll both benefit. If not, you won't lose anything."

Susan visited Nyakagyezi in 2005 and we worked together on the book for two years before our agent, Caitlin Blasdell, thought it was ready to market. The book sold to Viking-Penguin in a week and was released in June of 2010 as a hardback with the title, *The Price of Stones.* President Jimmy Carter touted it as "An inspiring account of turning tragedy into hope for others." USA Today called it "a moving memoir."

On June 14th, an article came out in *Time Magazine* entitled "Power of One," which described the founding of the school.

> "Twesigye Jackson Kaguri's American Dream was motoring along quite nicely until he was besieged by grandmothers. Born in a remote part of western Uganda, he'd studied hard enough to get to college in the capital, Kampala, and then to the U.S. He had an American job, an American wife and the beginnings of a down payment to buy a house."

I had been working at Michigan State for several years. Once the book arrived, I had to choose between keeping my university job or working for Nyaka full-time and going on tour. With encouragement from the board and from my good friend, mentor, and supporter, Tory Dietel, I took the *ente* by the horns and started travelling. The tour kicked off at local bookstores in East Lansing and Ann Arbor, but soon led me to Chicago, The Carter Center in Atlanta, and The Clinton School of Public Service at the University of Arkansas.

In December of 2010, I had just enough time to return to Uganda with Nic to visit family and attend the Nyaka graduation. After that, I visited Calvin College in Grand Rapids as part of their January Speaker series.

Calvin is a small Christian School with a modern campus surrounding a central park space. Everything was covered in snow that day. And, of course, it was COLD. My talk was at the Covenant Fine Arts Center, a large brick building with two stories of windows on the front, making it look a bit like a church.

I was greeted by Amy Patterson, Assistant Professor of Political Science. She was a thin woman with short-cut brown hair, glasses, and a friendly smile. Backstage, I was fitted with a microphone that wrapped over my ear and extended past my chin.

I had done plenty of public speaking by then, but I was always nervous before a talk. I peered around the corner into the auditorium and saw what had to be more than 200 people. I had assumed it would be mostly students, but there was a mixed crowd with plenty of gray hair.

President Gaylen Byker welcomed me. I shook his hand. In moments like these I always feel like that barefoot boy tending *embuzi* on the steep hillsides of Nyakagyezi. How amazed that little boy would be to know he would someday come to America and be greeted by the president of a university.

Dr. Byker preceded me to the podium. "It's my pleasure to welcome you to the January series of Calvin College. Please take a moment to silence your cell phones and pagers and then please join me in an opening prayer."

I bowed my head and thanked God that that little boy had come so far and was now able to give back to his village. After the prayer, Dr. Byker introduced Amy Patterson. She spoke about *Time* magazine highlighting my story as an example of how one person can make a difference in the world.

"It is not what you believe that counts," she quoted from my book, "It is what you believe you can do." She gave such a warm and thorough introduction that I worried she had delivered my entire speech in about five sentences.

"Thank you for that wonderful introduction," I said. "It is a huge blessing to be here." I joked with the audience about my Ugandan accent and said it was an honor to share my story. "Now, we are going to take a trip to Uganda and back again in the next hour."

I related my childhood, how my brother, Frank, had died from HIV/AIDS, and how I had come to build the school. Of course, I thought of my ex-wife when describing how we had used our savings to start the project, but it no longer choked me up as it used to. It had been almost three years. I had left married life behind and was happy being Nic's dad. Nyaka and the Nyaka kids were my life now.

My talk ended with Scovia's story, one of only a few Nyaka students born infected with HIV. When twelve-year-old Scovia was in the hospital dying from AIDS, she asked her grandmother if she could please be buried in her Nyaka uniform. Her *mukaaka* said they would make her a new dress, but Scovia insisted on the uniform because, in her much-too-brief life, she had been happiest at the school. That choked me up, as it always did, and still does.

"Nyaka is not a school," I said. "It is a life-changing place."

After the speech, I took several questions from the audience and had a book signing session in the atrium. To my surprise, I looked up to find Sara Ruiter, one of Nyaka's ardent supporters, standing before me, book in hand.

"Hello, Jackson." She brushed back her short blond hair and smiled. "That was a wonderful talk." She had come with one of her co-workers from Bethany Christian Services. "Now that you're finished with your engagement here, I expect you'll have time to consider our International Children's Conference in March."

It was not that I had been trying to avoid speaking at their conference, but the Christmas holidays and traveling to Uganda and back, had not left enough time. "Call me," I said. Two days later Sara set up an appointment to meet their leadership team and I was soon back on the highway, traveling from East Lansing to her office in Grand Rapids.

When I arrived, everyone was waiting—coordinators, managers, even the CEO. Despite Sara's endorsement, I was nervous. In the next hour I would have to convince this important group that Nyaka was an international story worthy of interest from their organization, justifying a speaker's fee.

I was being greeted by the usual handshakes and welcomes when a young woman with light brown skin and sparkling eyes entered the room. She extended her hand.

"*Eladde, ssebo*," she said in Luganda. "I'm Tabitha Mpamira." She smiled and the world opened. So shocked was I that I just stood there for a moment. Who was this beautiful woman? She must be from Uganda. How was it that Sara had not mentioned her?

"Hello," I said in English. "Good to meet you." Unfortunately, there was no time to talk further. I must remain professional.

I described for the group the founding of Nyaka and what we had accomplished since the school opened in 2003. At the end of the meeting I shook hands with the administrators and thanked them for inviting me. I could not tell whether they would invite me to speak at their conference. Sara seemed convinced the meeting went well, but I was less certain.

Tabitha Mpamira looked very serious when she approached after the meeting. "I want to tell you that I read your inspirational book," she said. "I was raised in Uganda like you."

"Near Kampala?" *Of course she is from the Kampala area, you fool.* That was why she spoke Luganda. She must have wondered how a man could build schools and write a book and not know his own country.

"I'm also Seventh Day Adventist," she said, being kind.

What? That was impossible.

I do not remember letting go of Tabitha's hand or what I said to anyone after that. All I could hear was my heart pounding in my chest. My head spun as I made my way back to the car and I was sweating despite the cold.

How could this be? After my divorce, I prayed and prayed to God to show me the way. Should I look for a new wife from the village? Should I date someone from the United States? Nothing seemed right. I was a man living in two countries and not fitting into either. I did not want to marry just because it was expected of me. I had Nic to consider, too, and did not want to make the wrong decision.

Just when I had decided to focus my life on Nyaka, the perfect woman stepped into my life. Had God waited all these years to answer my prayers? My mind whirled with confusion. I needed to talk to someone. At the time, my cousin, Samson, was my only blood relative living in the United States.

I called him as I drove home. "*Agandi*, Samson."

"*Nigye*," he said. "You don't usually call me in the middle of the day. What's wrong?"

I had forgotten the time difference between Michigan and San Diego. "Nothing," I said. "I had to talk to someone. I just met a woman."

"You're calling me in the middle of work because you met a woman?"

"Not just any woman." I followed I-96 past the airport. A plane rumbled above the highway.

Samson laughed. "I remember you saying you were never going to bother with women again. You were going to be a single man."

"Yes, I did say that." I had also told him he was smart not to get married. Being a single Navy man was a good choice for his life. I should have been smart like him.

"Are you sure you want to get involved with someone else?"

"She is perfect," I said. "She is Ugandan. She is Seventh Day Adventist."

"Mm," he said. "And where was she born? What tribe is she from? Who is her family?"

"I do not know," I said. "I just met her."

"You *do* know her name, don't you?"

"Of course," I said. Snow fell in large flakes. "Tabitha Mpamara. She shares a name with Mbabazi. Is that just coincidence?" To meet a woman in America with the same name, or part of a name, as my sister had to defy the odds.

"I think you should get to know more than her name before you decide to marry her."

Samson is right, I thought. I was being impulsive and lonely. I did not know anything about her. But I certainly wanted to know more.

NIWABIINE HILLARY

As a young boy, Hillary wanted to be an airline pilot, but as he grew older his interest turned to medicine. He scored high on national tests and was admitted to Ishaka Adventist College.

When the first student exam scores were posted for Senior-1. Hillary ranked 23rd in a class of 175. Hillary brought his class standing up to seventh by the end of Senior-1. During Senior-2 year, he conquered his shyness and began studying chemistry and physics with Fortunate, a Nyaka graduate who was first in the class. From then on, it became a competition between them.

During Senior-3, Hillary was first in the class three out of four quarters. He scored first in chemistry and received a 100% grade in physics. By Senior-4, he was first in the class the entire year. On the National Exams he made a 1st grade ranking, with distinction, and moved on to A-level to complete Senior-5 and -6.

Hillary received an acceptance from Kampala

International University School of Health Sciences in Ishaka. Medical training takes five years. He spent the first year studying basic sciences such as anatomy, physiology, and biochemistry. The second year included histology, pathology and pharmacology.

In July 2017, Hillary interned at Kambuga Hospital and the Nyaka Clinic, helping the only doctor working in the area. His dream is to be a heart surgeon.

CHAPTER 13

FATHER WOULD NEVER ALLOW IT

Following the Bethany Christian Services meeting, I asked Sara to send me email addresses for everyone who attended. Over the years, I have learned that a personal "thank you" is important. Many non-profit foundations are so large that they rarely speak directly with individual contributors. I wanted to make sure Nyaka would never be that way. Every contribution is important, be it $80,000 to build a school or $100 worth of pennies collected by a kindergarten class.

That evening, after a dinner of leftover pizza, I sank into the chair in my basement office. I do not normally send individual notes to everyone who attends a meeting, especially staff members. I send one "thank you" to the group, and maybe one to the director. This time was different. I had an ulterior motive.

Part way down the column, I saw Tabitha Mpamira's name. Maybe I was attracted to her because she reminded me of home, or because I spent my evenings alone in my big empty house when Nic was not with me, but I did not want to miss an opportunity.

I let out a long sigh and thought of my deceased sister, Mbabazi.

She had been a second mother to me when I traveled to Kampala to attend Makarere University. It was difficult to adjust to living in the big city, but she would always tell me to be brave. *You only have one life. You must make the most of it. Do not let things pass you by.* She died of AIDS with no regrets about her life. She would not want me to regret my decisions either.

"Be brave." I leaned forward and typed in Tabitha's email. I thanked her for attending the meeting and being interested in the Nyaka Programs. I told her it was a pleasure to meet her. It was more than a pleasure, but I didn't want to sound too anxious. I was careful to sound professional, but I did want to see her again. Asking her to dinner would probably be too forward. Then an idea came to me.

> I want to send you a signed copy of my book. What is your address?

I am thankful that I am a good sleeper. I can fall asleep two minutes after getting comfortable in an airplane seat. It makes long-distance travel easier.

That night I tossed and turned, waking up several times. I knew Tabitha would not answer in the middle of the night, but still I wanted to check for a response. I feared that she might not respond at all.

Morning finally arrived, and I was elated to see Tabatha's response. She was happy that I remembered her and wrote that she would love a signed copy of the book. No doubt she saw me as a successful author and school director who was being kind to a reader. She had no idea I wanted an excuse to see her again.

During our week of emailing back and forth, I learned that she was Rwandan and grew up in Uganda as a refugee because of the violence occurring in her country. Like me, she was one of five children, only she was in the middle of three sisters and a younger brother. Her family came to America in 1999, and she had studied psychology as an undergraduate and got an MA in Clinical Psychology.

Later, she confided to me that her parents had been in a tragic car accident the year before. Her mom died instantly, and her dad was in a coma for weeks. At the time of the accident she was working in Rwanda helping women who survived rape during the genocide. She gave up her vocation and moved back to the United States to take care of her dad and be with her family.

I told her I understood. Maama had been in poor health for years, suffering with a back injury. I always felt torn, wanting to live close to my family, and at the same time wanting to remain here in my new home. I was fortunate that my sister, Faida, lived close to my parents. She kept a watchful eye on them.

Tabitha asked if I would agree to be her mentor and help her set up a non-profit in memory of her mother. She gave me her phone number so we could speak directly.

I was in heaven. I could not tell her that, of course. I had only known her a couple of weeks and did not want her to get the wrong idea. She was several years younger than me, and her work had exposed her to the reality of predatory men. But the more I learned about her, the more I admired her. God had picked a match for me; I was sure of it. I would be patient.

Bethany Christian Services agreed to partner with Nyaka on a project, and I was invited to speak at their conference. That normally would have been enough to make me happy, but it was Tabitha's invitation to dinner at an Olive Garden in Grand Rapids that truly excited me. She saw it as a chance to discuss her non-profit. I could not think of it as anything other than a date.

When I arrived, Tabitha was waiting inside the door. The hostess sat us at a small table and set out the menus. I could not tell you what we ordered. The only thing I was aware of was that the food was served too fast. If we had been in Uganda it would take at least an hour, maybe longer, for the food to arrive. We would have had plenty of time to talk.

Tabitha was like a ray of sunshine on a cold Michigan morning. She told me about her yoga classes after work, how she liked Starbucks coffee and how much she loved flowers. Like me, she did her devotions every day. By the end of the meal I felt as if I had known her all my life. It was like visiting with a neighbor from the village.

When the discussion turned to my personal life, I was unsure what to say. I had to explain that many things had changed since the book was written. She had heard about the Kutamba school, the Blue Lupin Library, and Desire Farm during the Bethany meeting. What she did not know was that other things in my life had changed dramatically, as well.

I nibbled on a bread stick and tried to think of a way to ease into the conversation, but there was no simple way to say that my marriage had failed. I was a divorced man. I was probably the last man she should have any interest in. But I had to tell the truth.

"There is something I must mention," I said. "I am divorced."

"Oh," she said. "I see." I could not tell if she was upset. Did she think less of me? Was she reconsidering her interest in me as a mentor?

The waitress stopped by the table to refill our water glasses and ask if we needed anything.

"No," Tabitha said. "Everything is fine."

I was not so sure. This could be the last time I saw her, and I did not want that.

"I share custody of my son, Nic," I blurted. I was a good dad. She needed to know that. "He stays with me every three days. We like to go camping and hiking. I am his soccer coach."

She placed her fork on her plate and looked directly into my eyes.

"You must promise me one thing," she said.

"Anything."

"You must never hit on me," she said. "This is a professional relationship."

"Of course." I heard the worlds come from my mouth, but my heart was screaming otherwise. *This is the woman for you. Do not let her get away.* "I promise."

Being a man of my word, I kept my promise, but that did not keep me from falling in love with Tabitha. Our dinner meetings became more frequent. I would surprise her with Starbucks cards, flowers, and other small gifts. In two short months, she fell in love with Nic and he was just as fond of her.

Tabitha invited me to share the Nyaka story at her church, the Michiana Seventh Day Adventist in Berrien Springs. I met her dad, sisters, brother, and other relatives. We even had lunch at her dad's house. I felt comfortable with the whole family and they accepted me without question. Tabitha and I shared so much in common and got along so well, I am sure they thought we were dating. We certainly looked like a happy couple. But as far as Tabitha was concerned, we were just friends.

Finally, one night after we finished dinner at a local restaurant, I could not hide my feelings any longer.

"I know I promised I would never hit on you," I said. "I am

keeping my promise. But I did not promise that I would not marry you."

"Marry me?" She laid her napkin on her empty plate. "I don't have time for marriage," she said. "I still have to get my PhD. If the program in Texas accepts me, I'll be moving next year."

"You can get a PhD anywhere." I must make her at least consider the idea.

"That's not the point, I want to travel the world. I have a foundation to start. I can't be tied down."

"Being married does not have to stop you from doing any of those things. Look at me. I travel the country. I go to Uganda twice a year. I run a non-profit."

Tabitha took a sip of water. It was a logical argument. I hoped she was seeing things from my point of view.

"You're divorced," she said.

That stabbed me in the heart. Was that the real reason? Did she think something was wrong with me, that I had been an abusive husband? Did she think I was like my father?

"That is a totally separate issue," I said.

"Is it?"

"I am a good man. If we were married, you would be able to accomplish everything you want."

Tabitha shook her head. "No. We are good friends and I would like to keep it that way. I am not getting married."

All these years, I thought my father was the most stubborn person on the planet. Tabitha had him beat. It was obvious that we were happy together. I got along well with her family. She loved Nic. I was running out of things to convince her.

"At least think about it," I said. "I am not asking you to marry me tomorrow. I am not asking you to give up your identity. We can do this together, as a team."

"I don't think so," she said. "My father would never allow it. You're not Rwandan. You're divorced. And you're an older man with a son."

I took a deep breath and prayed. *God, I know you brought this woman into my life for a reason. Please give me the strength to make this work.*

AKANKWASA PRECIOUS

Akankwasa Precious went to Nyaka Primary School for primary education, then Ishaka Adventist College for four years.

After completing the Ordinary levels, she got married and dropped out of school. She has two children, both girls: Muheki Doreen, 6 years, and Kyobutungi Janet,-4 years.

CHAPTER 14

WE NEED TEAMWORK

At a time when I wanted to convince Tabitha to marry me, my book promotion schedule whisked me out of town. Carolyn Carlson, my editor at Penguin, used her connections to get me on a panel at the United Nations. I had thought the Clinton Foundation meeting was intimidating but it was nothing compared to speaking with international policy makers. On February 28, 2011, I was invited to be part of a special event entitled "Partnering with the Philanthropic Community to Promote Education for All."

H.E. Mr. Lazarous Kapambwe, the president of the Economic and Social Council, introduced the program. He spoke about the need for businesses to interface with non-profit groups to help assure that children around the globe get an education.

The U.N. program had several initiatives, including promoting education in countries devastated by HIV/AIDS, encouraging literacy, training teachers in Sub-Saharan Africa, and girls' education. They had already achieved goals in some countries, abolishing school tuition and fees in Nepal and Kenya, investing in teachers in Ghana, educating girls in Botswana, and expanding education in remote areas like Nyakagyezi. Their goals had been set in 2000, but Kapambwe said that the targets they had set for 2015 would not be met at the current success rate. More would have to be done.

Kapambwe continued advocating for ways to get children into the classroom and keep them there. He stressed innovation and the public and private sectors working together. "We need teamwork, and we need leaders," he said.

I surveyed the room while he ran a video entitled *Education for All.* I had seen TV footage of U.N. meetings and photographs of this very building. Now I was getting ready to step out and be part of a panel sitting on the main stage. How many world leaders had stood and delivered important speeches in this very room? The Nyaka Program was only one small organization. I could only hope that I would be able to add something useful to the topic.

After the introduction we joined our moderator, Ms. Daljit Dhaliwal, an International News Journalist, at a long table in the middle of the stage. At one end were Mr. Matthew Bishop, American Business Editor and New York Bureau Chief of The Economist, and Ms. Wendy Hawkins, Executive Director of the Intel Foundation. I sat next to Per Heggenes, CEO of the IKEA Foundation.

The moderator began with questions for Bishop and Hawkins. They made it clear that businesses contribute to organizations because they want something for themselves. Bishop said that businesses are often better at fixing things than governments. Hawkins stated that businesses understand the importance of education and the impact of primary and secondary education on the economy. Companies donate to educational causes "as an investment," not out of the goodness of their heart.

These comments struck me as cold and uncaring. Businesses like theirs would not see Nyaka as a school helping individual students who need love and security, but as numbers on a spreadsheet. Money goes in and employees come out like a factory producing TVs or cars. I did not admire this perspective, but non-profits were at their mercy. It took their attitude to create money, something they had in abundance and Nyaka lacked. It was important that I understand their view of the world, even if I did not appreciate it.

The moderator came to me next. "How do you engage with businesses when building schools for AIDS orphans."

"Ours is a little bit different from what you find in other places," I said. "We are located in a little village far away from everything that you would find in a city. So, we are working with students who are already orphaned in an area where you have nobody to invest in them. Many businesses are not there. You do not have Intel or Microsoft. You have small local businesses donating bricks. That is why my book is called *The Price of Stones*. We have little people each donating a little." I explained that once we were larger, we would need to partner with businesses to provide solar or water systems for the area.

Heggenes was interested in holistic approaches to education and tailoring educational systems to specific places. If we had been a larger organization, we might have been able to partner with him. In the end, I think I got my point across that children need food, a safe home, and healthcare if they are going to do well in school. I did not think I would find a business partner to help Nyaka School here. These people were looking for students they could hire. Heggenes supported schools in India, perhaps to employ the graduates in call centers.

Kapambwe had said the organization was not on track for achieving its goals by the 2015 deadline. I wondered if the business logic that philanthropy is just another investment was a reason for this lack of success. To me there is something missing when human kindness is removed from the equation.

On my flight home I thought of Nyaka students rushing out of their classrooms to greet me. *Director! Director!* They would laugh and dance and congregate around me for a hug. I always said hello to each and every one. I told them how proud I was and how sure I was that they would succeed. I was their Uncle, their Dad. They had suffered enough in their short lives. I was there to give them love unconditionally. There was no requirement for a return on that investment. Their happiness was more than enough.

As the plane landed in Detroit, I wondered if Tabitha was home. She would want to hear about the event. I could use that as an excuse to invite her to dinner. I would tell her all about the U.N. building and everyone I met. And even if she did not think we were on a date, I would consider it one.

MUGISHA IZIDOLO

Mugisha Izidolo went to Nyaka Primary School for Primary level. He went to Ishaka Adventist College for Ordinary levels.

After this, he attended Bishop Comboni College in Kambuga for Advanced level. He then went to Ndejje University in Luwero where he received a diploma in social work and social administration.

He graduated in October 2017 and lives in Nakasongola, where he works at Kabalega Dinner Restaurant as a procurement officer.

CHAPTER 15

HEALING OLD WOUNDS

After the success with sending Allan to Michigan for surgery, I was hopeful that we could find help for another Nyaka student who had been scarred in a terrible accident. The Shriners Hospital for Children in Boston volunteered to do the reconstructive surgery in 2011, three years after I first met Justine Nakunda.

When school lets out at the end of the day in the United States, kids rush to their busses eager to get home. Nyakagyezi students stay for an hour or more, depending on how long their walk is, often waiting until the sun has sunk below the horizon and olive ibises are flying from the river to their roosting places. Some take time to study, others talk to their friends, but the most popular pastime is playing soccer or netball. The local schools have teams which compete during the year. There are also student-teacher games, where the boys are challenged to beat the adults. Those were always my favorite games growing up and now as Director, I enjoy them even more.

In summer of 2008, after a two-day plane trip from the United States and eight-hour car ride from Kampala to the village, I was more than ready to give my legs a good workout. When I was invited to join the student-teacher game on the weekend, I told them I was up for the challenge. Those boys had better be ready.

Nyaka School does not have an area large or flat enough for an official field, so when we have competitions, we meet at another school up the road. Matt, the Kutamba architect, and Carol and Rob Auld were staying in the guest house that week but were too involved with Kutamba construction to attend the game. Chris Singer had arrived a few days before me. On that trip, he came as our resident photographer. Brittany Linville, a recent Indiana University graduate, teaching English to our students, rode with Chris and me in the van. She had her camera to take photos too.

Once word of the soccer game got out, it did not take long for the village to hear about it. There must have been a hundred people sitting in the grass waiting for the game to start. Nyaka boys arrived a few at a time from all over the area. They looked very professional in their team jerseys, but I did not plan to let them win. Some of the older girls on our netball team took advantage of the sports day and set up a game on the adjacent court.

I sauntered across the field to the teachers, showing the boys I had no fear of their talent. We strategized our defensive and offensive moves. Of course, I saw myself as a bit of an expert. I play regularly in Michigan and would show everyone a thing or two on the field. We decided to out-score the boys quickly then maybe take it easy for a while to let them get one point.

As the game began it was immediately clear that our plan was too simple. The boys had matured over the year, and some were almost better than me. They certainly kept me on my toes. For a while, I thought they were going to win.

While the crowd of mostly youngsters cheered and encouraged

the boys to beat the teachers, Chris spotted several boys teasing a girl in a faded flowered dress near the goal. The girl had a disfigured face. Burn scars stretched from her chin down her neck to her upper chest.

Nearby adults ignored the situation, which is not uncommon in the village. Many believe deformities are caused by evil curses and do not want to be affected themselves. They think it is best to stay away from people with physical maladies.

Chris, being the kind soul that he is, felt sorry for her. He approached the group. "Do you want me to take your picture?" He thought that might defuse the situation. The girl looked away. Brittany joined him.

"I can take your picture," Chris repeated.

"I don't think she understands English," Brittany said. "She's probably not in school and only speaks Rukiga."

"Oh," Chris said. "I didn't think of that." He had only been there a couple of days and had mainly interacted with Nyaka students.

"Picture," Brittany said, pointing to her camera.

"Yes. Picture?" Chris said. The teasing boys understood and posed between him and the girl. Chris ignored them. "You," he said to the girl. "May I take your picture?"

She nodded but could not smile. Her lower lip was pulled down by scar tissue so that her mouth was open all the time. Chris nudged the other kids out of the way and took a few shots.

"Me picture," a young boy in a grey t-shirt said.

Brittany took a few shots with her camera.

"Me. Me. Me," another girl begged.

"Okay," Chris said. "Line up." The kids pushed the girl back. "No," he said. "She's in the photo with you."

Suddenly, the girl's scars did not matter. Everyone was posing and making silly faces in front of the camera. When the soccer game finished, Chris and Brittany brought the girl to my attention.

"It looks like she was burned," Chris said.

I spoke to her and found out her name was Justine Nakunda. She lived in the village with her parents and siblings. The scars were the result of an accident. One night when she was carrying a lamp home, she tripped. Paraffin fuel spilled on her clothing and caught fire. With no specialized burn treatment in the village, the skin was left to heal naturally. Scar tissue extended along her neck and down her chest, forming a tight net. Along with pulling her mouth open permanently it prevented her from turning her head to the right or left.

"We should admit her to Nyaka School," Chris said.

"Her parents are alive," I said. "We cannot take everyone."

"But she's a special case."

"Most of the children in the village are special cases," I said. "If we could afford to educate all children in the village, we would do it."

"There must be enough money to support one more student," he said.

I looked over the soccer field. Barefoot village boys had joined the Nyaka students for another game. It was good to see them laughing and smiling. "If we only had one school," I said, "there might be something left over from last year's budget. But Kutamba will take everything we have."

Chris took photos of the boys.

"What will happen to her if she doesn't go to school?" he said.

I wanted to say *yes, we will enroll her,* but it was not my decision alone. That was why we had a board, headmaster and teachers. We worked as a team to evaluate every student.

"She should at least see a doctor," Brittany said. "She's never going to have a normal life unless something is done."

"You helped Allan," Chris said.

I wiped sweat from my forehead with my shirt. "Talk to the headmaster. See what he has to say. Then I will need to speak with the board."

The headmaster met Justine's family and she was accepted into the Primary-2 classroom that year. That solved part of the problem. Justine could have survived without facial reconstruction but as she neared puberty, we realized there was another matter to deal with. When her breasts began to develop, the scar tissue on her chest would not be able to expand. She was already 13 and looking at a painful development both physically and emotionally. Ruth, one of our nurses, offered to accompany Justine to America.

As expected, the American Embassy would not give Ruth and Justine visas. It was the usual excuse. The girls lacked enough ties to Uganda and would try to stay in the United States. All I could do was shake my head and tell them to try again.

During my next call with Carol Auld, she filled me in on the progress with Kutamba. I mentioned the visa situation.

"That's ridiculous," she said. "Are they blind? Can't they see that Justine needs surgical help?"

"I know," I said. "We had the same problem with Allan."

"I'll take care of it," she said.

Carol took Ruth and Justine to the embassy in Kampala, waited in the long line with them, and assured the woman processing applications that Justine was only going for medical treatment. "She has a family she loves in the village. It's obvious the girl needs treatment."

"Sorry," the woman said, handing her a new blank form. "We can't give her a visa at this time. Come back later."

Carol was not happy when she called. "They didn't want to listen to anything."

"We will just have to try again," I said.

"No, we won't," she said. "Let me make some phone calls."

Even though I avoid bribes in Uganda as a matter of principle, it is usually an advantage to know the right people. We were fortunate that Carol was able to pull some strings. Her daughter, Sara, went to school with Vanessa Kerry, John Kerry's daughter. A letter from the Massachusetts Senator turned the tide and Justine and the nurse got their visas.

Ruth Ndyabahika volunteered to host Justine in Boston. Ruth grew up in Chicago and Uganda and has always been involved in awareness campaigns such as Gulu Walks and the 2009 Uganda Lobby Day. A year after hosting Justine, she was inspired to found Grace Villa, a home and sanctuary for more than forty-five orphans and vulnerable girls from the hills of Kigezi. Grace Villa counsels and nurtures them while exposing them to unique programs.

Justine was wary of American food when she arrived but quickly became accustomed to the large variety of offerings, especially pizza and fries. Her primary job was helping her body to heal, but she did not miss out on her education. We wanted to make sure she would pass the national exams when she returned.

She worked with a tutor on decimals, adjectives, verbs, comprehension, and improving her reading skills. Her reading became so improved that she began to devour every book she could get her hands on. She also took up writing in a journal, easing the pain of the surgeries by keeping hilarious accounts of her new experiences. When she was not studying, she enjoyed arts and crafts and making jewelry. Even after Justine returned to Uganda, Ruth would find little gifts left around the house.

Justine spent nine months in Boston undergoing surgery and rehabilitation. I traveled to see her after she recovered, and she visited our offices in Michigan and our Friends of Nyaka group and Rotarians in Bloomington, Indiana. When her healing was complete, the doctors told her she might have to return if the scar tissue interfered with her breast development. She was monitored in Uganda and showed no signs of problems. This was good news for us, but Justine was a bit disappointed. She enjoyed her stay in Boston, but Harvard was in her dreams.

TURYATUNGA DENIS

Turyatunga Denis finished Nyaka Primary School and went on to do hair design and fashion in Kampala.

CHAPTER 16

AN UNDERSTANDING

Promoting the Nyaka Program had always kept me on the road, but 2011 was proving to be the busiest year ever. After returning from Uganda with Nic in January, I attended the U.N. meeting, Justine arrived in the United States for her surgery, and the Lansing group chose *The Price of Stones* as their reading book for the month.

The Mummy Drayton Clinic held its grand opening. I could not attend, but John Brewster, Paul Deweese, Betty Landegan, and Jennifer Natale were there. Several hundred people attended the dedication which included speakers, performances by students, and a traditional village feast with roasted goat, *matooke*, beans, cabbage, peanut sauce, and more. People were excited to tour the clinic.

After the grand opening, people lined up for dental check-ups from Dr. Brewster, many for the first time in their lives. Often the only service available in the village is a repair man with pliers who attempts to extract teeth. We provided John with a portable dental unit, dental chair, and air compressor. Because the equipment was mobile, he could also provide care to outreach clinics in the area.

During that first visit, two untrained assistants helped him. He was pleased that the students did not have more cavities, probably thanks to their low-sugar diet. The *mukaakas*, on the other hand, had many issues. He had to work to convince them that filling a tooth was better than an extraction.

Afterward, he lamented that he had not been able to do more. "I like to see as many people as possible," he said. With only two or three weeks to examine hundreds of people, he felt the approach had been less efficient than it could be. "We needed to be more organized," he said. "I mentioned it to Jennifer. Next year we will advertise beforehand on the radio."

He did train one of our nurses to do oral exams and clean teeth. In the future, he planned to bring along an oral surgeon. Between the two of them, they would be able to see about forty-five people a day, and deal with the more involved work such as fillings and extractions.

Over the next five years, John would vist both Nyaka and Kutamba as well as Kinkiizi Hospital. Several people accompanied him: Peter Hampl, an oral surgeon from Washington, Kim Schiiling, a dentist from New Mexico, Bosco Ekya, a physician assistant from Uganda, Terrie Erickson, a dental assistant from Oregon, Linda Schoenl, a nurse, and Bill Schoenl, from East Lansing.

As Spring 2011 approached, I spent as much time with Tabitha as I could. On one particularly warm day, as I was driving Tabitha back to her apartment, I noticed the snow had finally melted. The trees along the roadway were not yet leafing out, but the air smelled fresh and new. Maybe because I was tired of the long winter or because the season was changing, I decided to press the issue of our friendship.

Instead of dropping her off at her apartment, I asked if I could come inside. Tabitha agreed.

She lived on the ground level of a building near a grove of trees. Her apartment was small, especially compared to my rambling house, but it was clean and tidy. She had white couches with green and orange pillows and matching artwork that reminded me of Uganda. A basket of fresh fruit sat on the dining room table.

"Would you like something to drink," she asked.

"Water," I said.

She filled a glass from the tap.

"You are looking very serious," she said as she sat beside me. "Is something wrong."

"Everything is right," I said. "That is the problem."

"I don't understand."

"When we had dinner that first time, I promised not to hit on you. I have kept that promise, and more. But I want us to be more than friends."

Tabitha sighed. "I have already explained things to you, Jackson."

"You have said the words, but I do not believe that is what is in your heart." I sipped water. It tasted of chlorine. The chemical made water safer to drink than what we had in the village, but I could never adjust to the taste.

"How do you know what's in my heart?" Tabitha said.

"When we are together, you are happy. You laugh and giggle. Is that not what you feel? Are you not happy when we are together?" Her soulful brown eyes met mine. I wanted to kiss her more than ever but held back.

"I am an honest man," I said. "I will never hurt you."

"Mm," she said.

"I mean it. With all my heart, Tabitha." After getting her Master's degree in clinical psychology, Tabitha had returned to Rwanda after the civil war to help women who had survived rape. She had seen the worst side of men, men who beat their wives, men who rape young girls. I would never understand everything she witnessed but was convinced God brought us together for a reason. I had told her numerous times that I supported everything she was planning in her life, continuing her education and starting a foundation in memory of her mother. But that was not enough. As much as she seemed to enjoy being with me, there was always a wall between us, keeping her safe.

I leaned back on the couch and glanced out the sliding glass doors. Some people are easy to read. It is like looking through a windowpane. Others, such as Tabitha, are more complicated. How would I ever convince her that she was safe with me?

"We all have scars," I said. "I have a big scar where a piece of tree stump went through my leg. At the time, I thought I was going to die. There was blood everywhere and it took forever be carried to the hospital."

"I read about that in your book," Tabitha said.

"That scar is in the past," I said. "And easy to talk about. The other scars are up here." I pointed to my head. "Those are harder to deal with."

Tabitha touched my hand. I swallowed hard.

"My *taata* was a mean man when I grew up," I said. "He hurt me and my family deeply and often." I had tried to write about our relationship in my book but had not been able to face the entirety of it.

"Many men are that way," Tabitha said. "They feel they must be in control. That's the only way they know how to live."

I shook my head. "Taata did not need to be that way. My brother, Frank, was one of the kindest, most generous men I have ever known. He did not deserve... the beatings." Frank was much older than me. When he was a rebellious teen, he challenged my father.

I remembered Taata's voice booming through the house. He would yell at Frank, tell him how worthless he was, how he would not amount to anything. I huddled with my sisters, afraid that his wrath would spill into our sleeping room.

Frank raised his voice in turn. That was when the beating began. Taata would use whatever was on hand, a switch, a board, a fist.

Tabitha touched my cheek.

"He never had a kind word for anyone," I said. "Poor Maama. She stood up to his abusive language for years, but even she could not take it and left him for a while."

"She abandoned you kids with him?"

My throat pinched. I nodded. "He never beat Maama, but the rest of us were not so lucky. We never knew what would set him off. Not bringing the goats home on time. Wasting water. Taking too long to walk home or playing soccer after school."

"Isn't that why you built your own house?"

"It was the only way I could get away from him," I said. "The only way I knew to fight back."

Tabitha's eyes brimmed with tears. "No child should have to live that way."

"That is why I promised myself and God that I will never be like Taata. Thankfully, Freda, was there for me, especially when Maama was gone. If it had not been for her, I would not be talking to you today."

"We both have to thank God for saving us," Tabitha said. She stood and walked to the sliding doors. "My father was never abusive, but that did not...." She gazed across the yard. "I have never told anyone this."

I wanted to say something comforting but forced myself to sit quietly.

"I, too, was abused," she said in a whisper. "I was sexually assaulted when I was 11 years old."

"What?" Blood rushed to my cheeks. *Sexually assaulted?* Tabitha always came across as a confident, determined woman.

"He was a friend of the family."

Anger rose within me. I wanted to demand the man's name. I wanted to kill him with my bare hands. *Oh God*, I prayed. *Please forgive me.* It was not unusual to hear that some girl or woman in the village had been raped while walking to get water or running an errand. It was accepted as a fact of life. But not this woman, this precious, strong woman.

"I am so sorry," I said. The words sounded hollow, but I did not know what else to say. I wanted to go to her and hold her in my arms, tell her I would be her protector, but she would probably take it the wrong way.

"It happened a long time ago," Tabitha said. "I try not to think about it."

"But it stays with you," I said.

She nodded.

"I understand," I said. "You can talk to me anytime. You are safe with me."

"Thank you," she said.

PRECIOUS ATUSIIMIRE

I am Precious Atusiimire born in a village called Nyakagyezi in Kanungu district southwestern Uganda. I live there with my family that is uncle and auntie, my guardians after the death of my parents. Unfortunately, I lost my uncle recently due to uncertain circumstances. He left behind a family of nine members.

It has been such a big struggle ever since I lost my parents in terms of caring and supporting me and the rest of the children at home, especially in providing school fees and other scholastic materials due to the fact that we are many. My uncle used to pay fees in phases, meaning one or two had to go to school first because money was not enough, and others would go maybe a week later after getting money.

Honestly this was not such a good a story and life until one good Samaritan man came up with a plan and set up school for orphans in the village. I remember we were even in holidays and I did not know if I was going to report to school for the next term.

It was that hard time that advertisements started going through the whole village and churches that there's a new school for orphans. Me and my uncle went the day they were enrolling children to give it a try. Luckily enough, and I thank God, I was among the children that were enrolled to start school. The school was then opened officially where we started studying.

I started with Primary-1 to Primary-7 where I got my P.L.E certificate, whereby everything was provided including breakfast lunch, uniforms, shoes, books and pens and other scholastic materials. I completed Primary-7 thanks to the mercy, love and support of our well-wishers and sponsors, and did not stop.

From there I went for Ordinary level from Senior-1 to Senior-4 at Ishaka Adventist college in Bushenyi district where I got my U.C.E certificate in 2012. I went for my advanced level at Bishop Comboni College Kambuga where I got my certificate of U.A.C.E. I did well and was in position to qualify for higher studies at university.

I was enrolled at Makerere University where I pursued my honors of degree in education with arts under the scholarship and support of the Beautiful World Canada Foundation which facilitated me through all my years at the university including tuition, accommodation and upkeep among others.

Currently, I am not yet married and not working yet, but hope to get a job and start working and give back to others in need, especially to those students who are struggling with fees as I was once struggling, so that they can also get a chance to complete their studies and realize their dreams and live a life they are imagining, because hope begins with education.

Precious

CHAPTER 17

TYING THE KNOT

After visiting Uganda in January and attending the meeting at the United Nations in February, my book promotion tour for *A School for My Village* continued with readings, signings, and interviews. I traveled around the country from Massachusetts to Washington State.

Tabitha and I managed to grow closer despite this. By May, I could have let the relationship go on as it was, but why waste time? I set my sights on marriage. The first thing I needed to do was ask for her father's blessing. She had told me he would never approve. I was sure I could convince him.

I was nervous when I invited him to lunch and even more nervous when we sat across the table from each other. He was a humble, hardworking, God-fearing man, and I had come to respect him for what he had accomplished in life. I hoped he saw me as honest and responsible, but tradition was important.

I ordered food, and we talked about many things, but my mind was not on the conversation and I could not tell you what we ate. I do remember the knot in my stomach when the meal was finished.

I practiced the words in my head. *Will you give me your blessing? I would like to marry your daughter. I know I am divorced, but I promise to be a perfect husband.*

"There is another reason I asked you to lunch," I finally said. My heart pounded. "I want your blessing to marry your daughter."

"Who?"

"Your daughter. Tabitha."

He smiled, and I realized he was joking with me.

"I..."

"You want my blessing?" He leaned back in his chair and looked me over. "You were previously married?"

"Yes," I said. This would be the beginning of many questions.

"You were married only once?"

"Yes."

His eyes narrowed. "There are no other wives here or in Uganda?"

"No," I said. Some men in Uganda are polygamous. My grandfather had had several wives before converting to the Seventh Day Adventist religion. "Only one ex-wife."

"And you have just one son from that marriage?"

"Yes," I said. "Nic."

"And what of your ex-wife? Where is she?"

"She lives in Okemos."

Her father took a drink of water. "And where does your son live?"

"We share custody," I said. "Nic takes turns staying at my home."

"Are there any problems with the custody?"

"No," I said. "We have a good relationship. Nic is well taken care of."

"And what did Tabitha say when you asked her to marry you?"

"I have not asked her yet."

His eyebrows raised. "You did not ask her first?"

"No," I said. "I wanted your blessing."

He nodded. Apparently, he appreciated my gesture of respect. I braced myself for more questions.

"You have my blessing," he said. "As long as Tabitha agrees. We will prepare for a *gusaba*."

I knew now that everything was going to follow Rwandese culture. *Gusaba* means "to ask" and is a traditional ceremony for those who intend to marry. First, there is a *gusaba*, then a civil marriage usually followed by a church wedding. During *gusaba*, elders from the groom's family lead an entourage of relatives to the bride's family to ask for the daughter's hand in marriage for their son. Elders from the groom's family engage in a battle of wits with their counterparts from the bride's family. The event usually includes a dowry payment before the girl's family officially gives her hand in marriage.

Traditional dress is worn, the bride wearing an *umushanana* or a sari. The groom and his entourage used to go bare-chested but today usually wear silk shirts and a two-piece wrap with necklaces and leather sandals. There is also a poet to recite a poem for the cows and families usually try to outdo each other in the recitation. The traditional beer, *Ikigage,* has been replaced by modern liquors or even soda. Instead of dancers, some people hire a musician to spice up the event.

Tabitha's father did not have any other questions, which was a big relief. Next on my list would be the proposal. I wanted it to be special, something Tabitha would always remember.

Spring in Michigan was cool and wet, as usual. It was the perfect excuse.

"I have an idea," I said to Tabitha. "We both have time off for the Memorial Day holiday. Let's go south for a long weekend and spend time on the beach."

"That does sound wonderful," she said. "But I don't know if I can afford..."

"I will pay the entire cost."

She agreed and my chest swelled. Confident that she would accept my proposal, I stopped at a Jared jewelry store and bought a ring. If Tabitha suspected anything, she did not show it.

We stayed in a Gulf Shores hotel right on the ocean. The day of the proposal, I spoke to the hotel reception staff and arranged a surprise. We went out to dinner. On our way back to the room, we discovered rose petals sprinkled in the hall.

"What is this?" Tabitha asked.

I shrugged and unlocked the door. Inside, flowers and champagne waited on the table.

"Jackson!" Tabitha said. "What are you up to?"

I felt the ring box in my pocket. This was the woman who said she was not looking for a relationship just a few months before. There was a chance she would reject my proposal, but I had been praying every day that I was on the right path. Why would God introduce us if He did not mean us to be together?

I knelt to one knee and opened the ring box. Tabitha looked stunned. Tears ran down her beautiful face.

"Tabitha," I said. "Love of my life, I have been waiting to ask you. Will you marry me?"

"I..."

"I have already asked for your father's blessing."

She trembled, eyes glistening.

"And I bought a ring," I said. "You have to say yes."

She laughed. "Yes."

I slid the ring onto her finger. We hugged and embraced for a long time, kissed, and toasted our future life together. I was relieved, happy, excited, all at the same time.

When we returned to Grand Rapids, I checked on government marriage ceremonies. They were performed at the Kent County Courthouse on Thursday afternoons. We got our license and had a civil service on June 2nd. Judie, Tabitha's sister, and Damarie, a friend of mine from Uganda, were our witnesses. We dressed up for the occasion. I wore a gray suit and tie and Tabitha donned a matching silver-gray dress with a flower on the shoulder. Still, the ceremony was cold and official. We looked forward to the *gusaba.* Tabitha insisted that we also have a regular wedding with the white dress and everything.

After the civil wedding Tabitha quit her job and moved into my home. Her dad reserved a location for the *gusaba* at the end of June at Fernwood Botanical Gardens, southwest of Grand Rapids along the St. Joseph River. The gardens were beautiful with all the greenery and flowers. There were trails, a waterfall and large pond on the property. It was a perfect spot for the celebration.

Ruth brought Justine to the Rotary meeting on June 23rd, so they were in town for the *gusaba.* It was a large affair, with some of our friends and family in the United States attending, over 60 people in all. Tabitha and I chose traditional clothing. She wore a golden two-piece dress trimmed with silver sequins. Her hair swept upward into rolling curls and a beaded headband crossed her forehead. I wore a plain white shirt and a wrap of two layers of material, leopard print and sheer white, that reached almost to my feet.

The celebration featured a huge feast of African foods. Steamed *matooke*, rice, beans, cabbage, *posho*, groundnuts, goat, chicken and so much more. I wished that Maama, Taata and my sisters could be there, but we had just dealt with getting visas for Justine and Ruth. There was no way to get my family to the United States in time.

I did hope that some of my family might get visas to attend the church wedding ceremony later in the year. Tabitha's sister, Grace, had held her wedding in Jamaica where visa restrictions were not such a problem. We decided Puerto Rico would be a nice place for a wedding. Tabitha began to make plans.

Those plans were postponed when we received the next surprise. At first, I thought Tabitha was sick with the flu. She was not feeling well and had an upset stomach. Instead of passing in a couple of days, it got worse, and she began throwing up in the morning. I began to worry.

"I'm pregnant," she said.

Pregnant? I was overjoyed. I would be a dad for the second time. I would have another son, or maybe a daughter this time. In the same moment, I thought of my promise to Tabitha. How would she go to graduate school with a baby on the way?

"Are you happy?" I asked.

"Yes," she said.

"What about your education and the non-profit?"

She pressed her palm to her stomach. "We'll work it out."

NAMANYA HELLEN

Namanya Hellen completed Nyaka Primary School. She then went to Ishaka Adventist Secondary School.

After Senior-4 she attended Makerere Institute, Rukungiri. She currently works as a house maid in Tanzania.

CHAPTER 18

A FEASIBILITY MEASURE

After dinner, I usually retire to my desk in the basement office. Everything is quiet and I can collect my thoughts. As more and more Nyaka students became teens with teenage problems, it was becoming increasingly difficult to focus. The oldest students were now at secondary school in their Senior-3 year. Since they left Nyakagyezi, three girls had become pregnant. Three students had been suspended from school. One boy thought it necessary to steal food and sell it to other students in his dormitory. *Thou shalt not steal.* Had we not taught him the fundamentals?

All the Nyaka students were my children, and I felt guilty that I could not be there for them. It was obvious that some were not ready to leave home. They were teased for being AIDS orphans, too far away for family to visit, and did not have enough emotional support. There was no granny to watch over them, no auntie to help the girls through difficult times. The holistic approach we used at Nyaka was not being carried forward. I was getting desperate.

I had mentioned building a secondary school to the Board of Directors during a couple of conference-call meetings. Each time, they acknowledged the issue and then dropped it. Nyaka was not ready for such an undertaking. We had barely completed Kutamba. The farm needed upgrades.

I also spoke with previous donors. One said she was worried about Nyaka growing so quickly we would be unable to meet expectations. Another said they did not fund building projects.

I understood these points of view. Even so, my heart ached for the kids. I remembered the sweet faces of our founding class on their first day of school. They were so excited they could not keep from giggling.

As they returned each year, they knew we had high expectations, but we also loved them unconditionally. We were there for them every step of the way, good and bad. I could not desert them now.

I am proud of the Nyaka Board of Directors, those serving and those who served before them. We have always had a diverse and thoughtful group, from bankers to fund managers, teachers, lawyers, and doctors. They have provided a much-needed backbone for our organization. We have a face-to-face meeting once a year, and they do not hesitate to give me advice.

Our 2011 meeting was held in the New York apartment of one of our members. Emma Mugisha and Frank Byamugisha flew in from Uganda. Dr. Jude Mugerwa, a native of Uganda now practicing cardiology in the United States, arrived soon after. Two long-standing supporters, Cath Inanir and Barbara Kroberger, joined us from Turkey and Philadelphia respectively. Others came from as far as Colorado.

The board had dropped the issue of a secondary school in conference calls, but now that we were face-to-face I was determined to press the subject. I could not continue to spend my evenings worrying about the safety of our boys and girls. We needed to be there for them.

Janis Simon was our board chair at the time. She had taught art in public schools and is the mother of five grown children. I met her through the Segal Family Foundation, but soon discovered she was involved with several other organizations. It had been her idea to provide students with breakfast as soon as they arrive at school because many live so far away and are tired and hungry when they finally get there. That had proved a very fine idea, since it helped our students to focus on their studies.

Janis had travelled with me and without me to Nyaka. She met with major donors, hosted events at her homes in Chevy Chase, Maryland, and Vail, and even convinced her brothers and sisters to give. She also sat on the board for Segal Family Foundation, which was on its way to becoming Nyaka's largest donor.

Janis' husband, Ronny Simon, joined us. A natural leader, he had operated a successful roofing contracting business for many years before selling it. Extremely financially savvy, he knew all the codes, always reviewed our books, and advised us on construction-related matters. Thus, we had two great people for the price of one.

After we covered pressing business issues, I braced myself for what could be a spirited debate.

"I want to talk about the secondary school again," I said.

"Of course," Janis said.

I had been thinking about ways to convince the board all morning. I began with a comparison.

"A tree has to have deep roots if it is going to grow," I said. "Our students are like trees. If we feed and water them, they will send roots deep into the ground. They will have a strong foundation on which to grow.

"I know a secondary school will cost more than we have ever spent, but I feel our students are not being given the foundation that they need. We educate them for seven years and let them go. Part of what we have taught them is erased completely on those long rides to other districts."

I expected to see signs of disagreement, but everyone listened intently. My sense of dread lessened.

"We are sending most of our students to Ishaka. They are getting into trouble. One was even jailed. Boys from other areas are tempting our girls into having sex for gifts of phones and clothes. Some have been raped and impregnated."

"We can't protect them entirely," Barbara Kroberger said. "But something needs to be done."

Paul Deweese offered concerns about our financial stability.

"It is costing $500 a year to send a student to secondary school," I said. Sara Dunkley of Beautiful World Canada had been paying students' high school and college tuition since 2010. "If we build a school, we can educate them at a much lower cost. We can also enroll students from outside the Nyaka program. A secondary school will pay for itself once construction is all done."

"Kanungu District is home to many of the poorest Ugandans," Cath Inanir said. "There is no running water, very little electricity. How do you expect to find students to enroll in this school?"

"People will find a way to pay," I said. "Like my parents did."

Cath looked doubtful.

"Every Ugandan wants their children to have an education," Emma said. She grew up in Buyaja, a small village near Rukungiri Town across the Enengo from Nyakagyezi. Now she is a banker at Stanbic Bank. "Nyaka educates the poorest of the poor, but many farmers are able to sell goats, cows, or land to ensure their children receive an education."

"Emma is right," Frank said. "And not all the money comes from Kanungu District. I am from Rugyeyo, but now that I work for World Bank in Washington D.C., I am able to send money back to my village."

"And you think there would be enough interest in the school?" Cath asked.

"People want to enroll their children in Nyaka Primary School because of its reputation," I said. "Our students have some of the highest national test scores. It will be the same with a secondary school. People know Nyaka means quality."

"There will be a large upfront capital investment," Paul said.

"Yes, of course," I said. "But it will offset our annual operating costs. Each year Nyaka and Kutamba schools graduate a class of sixty students." I had multiplied that figures in my head over and over again. "That is thirty thousand dollars per year. Three years of senior level classes equals ninety thousand dollars. Building, maintaining, and managing our own school should be a fraction of that. We can also recruit donors to help pay Nyaka student costs."

"If we decide to do this," Diane Hunckler said, "we will need a feasibility study. I want to see resource and capital requirements, a fundraising strategy, and financial analysis."

"Of course," I said. Diane and her husband William had their own foundation and were keenly aware of the financial issues that we faced.

Inside, I was cheering. The board had not dismissed the idea out of hand.

Ann Hopkins and Chris Lowe suggested we hire someone to establish a fundraising plan. Jennifer Thomson nodded in agreement. She had degrees in public and international affairs and was involved with micro-finance.

"I can do that," I said. "There is no reason to spend more money than we have to."

KYOKUSIMA MOREEN

Kyokusima Moreen completed Primary-7 from Nyaka Primary School. She joined Ishaka Adventist but dropped out in her fourth year of secondary school.

She is married and has two children. Tragically, one died.

She lives in Entebbe and sells *matooke* and tomatoes to help support her family.

CHAPTER 19

NOT THE ONLY CNN HERO

2012 began with the birth of our son, Nolan. Tabitha had been so sick during the pregnancy, I worried about her and the baby every day. No one was happier than I to see he was healthy and strong. I thanked God for protecting them both.

I wished I could have stayed at home more, but I was busy running the Michigan office, communicating with the Kampala office, scheduling fundraisers, and contacting donors. At Nyaka, we were installing a second clean water system. We were also breaking ground for another Blue Lupin Library at Kutamba, building a new storage shed at the farm, and treating hundreds at the clinic each month. The Grandmothers Program was expanding, and Kutamba would be graduating its first class in December.

In February, I had a book talk and signing at the East Lansing Public Library and an interview with Shannon Ritter of *Profiles.* I was always in the car traveling to one place or another. It was during a trip across town that I took a call on my cell phone. I did not recognize the number, but that was not unusual.

"Hello," I said.

"Hello," a woman answered. "Is this Jackson Kaguri?"

"Yes."

"This is Allie Torgan with the CNN Heroes program."

"What?" I almost ran the car off the road. Fortunately, the weather was warm for a Michigan winter. I did not hit ice as I veered toward the curb and swerved back into the lane.

"I'm Allie Torgan from CNN."

Okay. Calm down, I thought. I spotted a place to park and turned off the street into a lot.

"Ah, hello."

"I am calling to inform you that you have been nominated and selected to be one of our Heroes this year."

I never thought of myself as a hero, just a man helping his village. Several people had put my name in for the Hero program over the last few years, but I thought the competition was too steep for a small program like Nyaka.

"Thank you," I said.

"Don't thank me yet," she said. "We had about 10,000 applications to choose from, and yours looks promising, but this is only the beginning. We are a professional news agency, and we must investigate you and your organization to establish the facts. Once we are sure that we have all your information, the Hero award will be finalized."

"Oh, okay," I said. This sounded serious.

"We will need to see financial records as well as your personal tax records. After that, we will request references of people to interview. If all that works out, then we will go to Uganda to see the program. Do you still want continue?"

"Sure." I had nothing to hide.

My mind whirled as she outlined the process. It would take

months for them to investigate me and Nyaka thoroughly, and I was told not to mention it to anyone until the award was announced. I did not know how I could go that long without telling anyone. I had to at least tell Tabitha.

Allie must have been hearing my thoughts. "Do you want to know who nominated you?"

"Yes, please."

"Your wife, Tabitha Kaguri."

"What?" I laughed. She had not given me any indication, not one clue.

"I'm sure she'll be happy to hear the news," Allie said.

"Yes, yes she will."

I called Tabitha right after Allie said goodbye.

"I just got a phone call from CNN," I said.

Tabitha shrieked with happiness. "I didn't want to tell you. I didn't want to raise your expectations."

It took weeks to get all the information submitted and the interviews completed. CNN representatives wanted to speak with a Ugandan government official, so I recommended the prime minister, Amama Mbabazi. He was from Kihihi, a town near Nyakagyezi, and knew all about the program and what we had accomplished. He would put in a good word.

The interview with Amama was a success. Allie informed me that they would travel to Nyaka next.

A few weeks later, I met them in Kampala. We drove to the village where they spent three days visiting the schools and filming for a video. When they left, I felt that I had represented the program in the best way I could. The CNN team seemed impressed with everything we were doing.

After passing their inspection, I was informed that I would be one of the nominees. Next, my story would be posted on their webpage. They interviewed me and combined that with some of the footage they had taken in the village. When they were finished, they had a piece that was one minute and forty seconds long. This would be all that the world would see when my nomination was announced.

I hoped what I said would be enough to hold people's attention. "In Uganda, HIV came striking like a machete in a corn field," I began, "killing men and women and leaving 1.2 million children orphaned." The video included footage of the grandmothers, the kids and the schools. They scheduled it to be released in June. More interviews and book signings followed, which was good since a busy schedule keeps one from dwelling on a competition. In May, I was the keynote speaker at the Global Fund for Children (GFC) Gala in Manhattan.

The GFC was founded by Maya Ajmera in 1993. She is a slim, dark-haired woman, well-spoken and very bright. We first met at a conference in 2005. That meeting led to Nyaka's first grant for $3,000 from GFC. Each year their grant increased until we reached $7,000 five years later. After that, we were supported with a one-time $25,000 sustaining grant.

Maya was a true hero. She believed that small grants given to innovative, community-based organizations could impact the lives of the world's most vulnerable children. In two years under her leadership, GFC increased its grant-making budget tenfold. By its tenth anniversary, it was helping organizations thrive by providing management support, technical assistance, and networking opportunities. The education and training they provided us was an important factor in Nyaka's success.

We had received our final grant from GFC earlier in the year.

Now that we were considered self-sustaining, GFC would use its money to help other emerging organizations. I was there to thank them for their help, show them what Nyaka had accomplished, and encourage donors in the audience to keep giving their money.

The GFC gala attracted many of New York's wealthiest, a who's who list of elite donors. Tables covered with white tablecloths greeted more than 400 guests. Food and drinks were plentiful. Women wore designer evening gowns, men name brand suits and shoes.

"Excuse me," an older woman said as she entered the room. "Are you part of security?"

"No," I said.

She nodded and scanned the room, looking for someone. She apparently found them for she quickly moved between tables toward the front of the audience. I looked down at myself. I'd worn my best black suit and gray tie. Could she tell I was not wearing an expensive designer garment with just a glance? Did I look like staff? In Uganda, guards always wear uniforms so they are easy to identify. I shrugged it off and moved toward the stage.

Kristin Lindsey, CEO of the organization, took the stage first. Spotlights reflected from the white scarf draped over her shoulders. She was an older woman. From her accent I gathered she was not a native of the African continent, but probably an African American.

She spoke about the war in northern Uganda and Joseph Kony kidnapping children as servants and soldiers. From that point, she broadened her talk to include many countries around the world where GFC was helping small non-profits make a difference.

She ended with two important statements. First, that grass roots organizations are worth investing in. Second, that "we are all very lucky people." I glanced around the room. I hoped this audience appreciated what she said. They were more than lucky. For less than the price of one pair of their shoes, I could send a Nyaka student to a secondary boarding school for a year.

After Kristin's speech, a couple came up for an award. I saw the woman who had questioned me earlier at their table. She must be the mother of one of them. She was certainly surprised when I was introduced as the keynote speaker.

I stepped to the podium. A slideshow of photos of kids from Nyaka and Kutamba schools projected onto the screen beside me.

"Good evening," I said. "Thank you for having me."

After pleasant applause, people sat quietly at the tables. I found Maya in the crowd. She had started the organization at such a young age that she still looked like a college student. She flashed a smile.

"I know two people who want to grow up to be like each other," I said. "I tell myself all the time that when I grow up, I want to be like Maya. She says when she grows up, she wants to be like Jackson. That maybe makes us twins." The crowd responded with a laugh, and I relaxed.

"It is an honor and pleasure to be speaking to you," I pointed to the photos behind me. "The voice you hear is not Jackson Kaguri's voice, but the voice of children in a tiny village in Uganda being represented here at this gala." I spoke of Nyaka's progress, and how instrumental GFC had been in our success. I encouraged donors in the crowd to give. The program worked for us, and there were millions of children around the world who needed their help.

It was an excellent evening, and I felt more inspired than ever.

My CNN Hero Award was announced on June 22nd in an article by Allie Torgan, and the video they had created was broadcast for five days straight on CNN. I was one of 24 heroes to be recognized that year.

In December, votes would be held to determine the top ten heroes, who would each receive $50,000, and a single hero of the year who would receive $250,000. I had to admit it would be nice to win the award money but when I discovered who the other heroes were, I felt they were at least as deserving.

Pushpa Basnet started a children's center that provided housing, education, and medical care to more than 140 children of incarcerated parents in Nepal. Catalina Escobar provided counseling, education, and job training for teenage mothers in Columbia. Razia Jan was making sure girls in rural Afghanistan had access to education. Malya Villard-Appolon had co-founded KOFAVIV, an organization that has helped more than 4,000 rape survivors.

Clearly, I was not the only hero.

HANNINGTON BYAMUKAMA

Hannington is 29 years old and has one child, a daughter named Devin. He lives in Kawempe, a Kampala suburb. He is a double orphan since his mother passed away in 2018.

He Joined Nyaka in 2003 when he was in Primary-2 and completed his primary education in 2008.

In 2009 he proceeded to join Gables Vocational Institute and did a two-year course in Motor Vehicle Mechanics. The same year (2011) he completed his course, he started working with Nyaka. He is still working for Nyaka as a driver based at the Kampala Office. He has worked with

Nyaka AIDS Orphans Project for eight years. Hannington was married in August 2019.

CHAPTER 20

WOMEN AND GIRLS

Nolan's arrival into the world made planning a wedding with a white dress and all the trimmings more difficult, but Tabitha managed to pull things together. In July we boarded a plane for Puerto Rico with the boys.

El San Juan Hotel was not far from the airport and sat a few paces from a pristine white-sand beach. The ocean beyond reflected in brilliant turquoise, quite a contrast to lakes in Michigan which tended to be olive-green or dark blue.

The hotel was modern, with four restaurants and a little coffee bar called the *El Cafecito*. The most striking feature was a pool area between the building and the beach. Not one pool, but three, each bordered with lounge chairs and cabanas. The pools wound around islands covered with ferns and palm trees.

After we checked into the wedding suite, Tabitha and I strolled around the pools and exited through a gate to the beach. Nolan had stayed with the babysitter, but Nic went straight for the water.

"It's perfect," Tabitha said.

We waded through shallow ripples. As far as I was concerned, any place was perfect if Tabitha was with me.

Guests arrived. Some stayed at el San Juan, others at a bed and breakfast. In all, 45 people came. My guests included Ingrid Scott from the United Kingdom, Promise and Cath from Turkey, Jude Mugerwa with his wife and boys, and my cousin, Samson from San Diego. All three of Tabitha's sisters, her brother, and their families, her father, cousins, aunts, and a few family friends invited by Tabitha attended.

The next morning, I went out for a run on the beach. Multi-story hotels and pools of various sizes and shapes crowded the coastline. Seabirds squawked overhead and circled the buildings. A tanker sailed along the horizon. Signs advertised snorkeling and jet skiing, but these businesses were not open yet.

When I returned, I found Jude, Samson, and some of the other guests lounging in the pool area.

"Did you see the movie crew on your run?" Jude asked.

"No." I looked back. I had only encountered about a dozen people.

"They are shooting a movie right down the street."

"Really?" I said. "Any big stars?"

"I saw Ben Affleck," Samson said. "I'm sure it was him."

"You are joking me."

"No. They're two blocks that way." He pointed.

Before long, everyone was talking. We discovered that Ben Affleck and Justin Timberlake were filming scenes for the movie, *Runner Runner.* Hotel staff informed us that the movie crew had even used a suite at our hotel as a backdrop.

"Let's go see them," Samson said.

"Sure," I said. "Why not?"

We walked along tree-lined sidewalks to the filming site. The road was blocked, and a guard stood watch. We stopped there and watched from a distance. I am pretty sure I glimpsed Justin Timberlake, but that was as close as we were going to get to the Hollywood stars.

After our brief excursion, I turned my attention to the wedding. The hotel set up chairs trimmed in pink and orange on the beach. Tables were readied for the dinner, but we had to settle for American food rather than traditional *matooke* or *posho.*

The next day, my dear friend Ingrid Scott took to the podium to officiate. Nic was my best man. We wore tan suits and white shirts with pink ties. Tabitha had even found a matching outfit for Nolan.

Her sister was maid of honor. She came through the gate and walked down the sandy aisle first. Tabitha was a gorgeous bride at our civil wedding, unbelievably beautiful at the *gusaba*, but as she glided toward me in that white dress, it was as if an angel had come to earth. I was the happiest man alive.

Our celebration went late into the evening, with plenty of food, cake, music, and dancing. A half-moon rose high in the sky. Stars sparkled against the darkness. Tabitha and I strolled along smooth sand, waves winding between our toes. I was a successful man with a beautiful, intelligent wife, two brilliant sons, and a promising future. I thanked God for my bounty.

Before I knew it, the sun was rising, and it was time to return to cold, wet Michigan. Still, it was different from other plane rides. That afterglow of contented joy would not soon leave. I held Tabitha's hand even as my thoughts turned to the busy schedule of interviews, talks, and radio shows ahead.

Back at the Nyaka office, I received an invitation to speak at the annual gala for the *60 Million Girls Foundation* in Montreal, Canada. I had been introduced to the organization's founder through the Stephen Lewis Foundation a few years before.

Not only was Wanda Bedard an amazing engineer, she owned a Canadian custom sheet metal company that built nuclear shells for the Canadian government. A decade before, she became interested in the world's vulnerable children and volunteered with UNICEF. There she developed projects, organized activities, and ran fundraising campaigns. In 2006 she and a small group of women established the *60 Million Girls Foundation.* We met and she became so interested in what we were doing in Nyaka that she came to visit the school with her two daughters.

Each year, Wanda's organization raises money for a different non-profit group and partners with the Stephen Lewis Foundation to distribute the funding. This year they had chosen *Free the Children,* a Canadian-based organization that supported more than 55,000 children in 45 developing countries. Roxanne Joyal, the *Me to You* organization's co-founder, would also be speaking at the conference.

I looked forward to the event and hoped that they would support Nyaka in the future. The secondary school was still on my mind, and it was going to take the biggest investment we had tried to raise yet. School rooms, laboratories, and computer labs, trade school rooms, dormitories, and a cafeteria would cost more than the Nyaka and Kutamba schools combined. There were eight buildings in total. I had it all in my head. Sam Ampumuza had drawn the plans. And, on top of that, we still had our primary students to support.

Now that the wedding was behind us, and Nolan was nine months old, I encouraged Tabitha to think about going back to school for her PhD. I suggested we find a nanny to care for Nolan. She liked the idea.

In September, however, she started getting sick in the morning. *It must be a flu or an infection*, I told myself. You would think I would know better by now. The sickness continued.

"I'm pregnant again," she informed me.

Oh my, I thought. God was bestowing too many blessings upon us now.

Tabitha had been sick with her first pregnancy, but this time was much worse. Some days she could not eat. She would spend hours in bed and became so dehydrated I had to take her to the hospital for IV drips every few weeks.

"I am so sorry," I said. This was not what I had in mind when I asked her to marry me. Not only was she not able to attend school, but I feared for her health.

"It's not your fault," she said. "God blessed us with a healthy son. This pregnancy will end well, too. I'm sure of it."

She may have been sure, but I fretted every day. Local events like the *Live Chat* I did with Brian Wheeler in East Lansing did not worry me much. It was close to home and if Tabitha needed me, I would not take long to get to her. The *60 Million Girls* Annual Gala in Montreal was another matter. Not only would I be far away, I would be out of the country. If something happened to Tabitha, I did not know what I would do. I prayed to God constantly. *Please, help her through this pregnancy.*

I always travel to Uganda the last week in December, but this year I was torn. I needed to meet with Nyaka teachers and staff and visit with my family, but a one way trip would take three days. If Tabitha had to go to the hospital, I would be lucky to receive a phone call in the village, and it would be impossible to get home quickly.

"I do not think I should go to Uganda this year," I said.

"I'll be fine," she said. "My family is here. If there's a problem, my sisters will help me."

"I do not want to leave you."

"What about the Nyaka kids? They need you, too."

In the end, I made the trip early in December, so I could be home for Christmas. Tabitha was right, as always. She survived without me. Shortly after I returned, we had an appointment for an ultrasound. Tabitha had eaten so little I did not know how the baby could survive. I prepared myself for the worst.

The technician ran the probe over Tabitha's belly.

"There," she said, pointing to the grainy image. "Foot one. Foot two. Foot three. Foot four."

Tabitha looked puzzled.

"What?" I said.

"Didn't you know? You have twins." She moved the probe. I saw one round head and then a second one.

Twins! No wonder Tabitha was so sick.

"Do you want to know the sex of the babies?"

"Yes," Tabitha said. She grabbed my hand.

I nodded. Nolan was not even a year old and we would have two more babies by spring. How were we going to manage that? How were we going to afford two more children? I was elated and terrified at the same time.

"This one is a girl," the technician said. She adjusted the probe. "And the other one is...a girl. You have twin girls."

AGABA DELICK

Agaba Delick completed P-7 from Nyaka Primary School. He went to Ishaka Adventist Secondary School, but was expelled.

He then went to St. Charles Lwanga in Zorooma, where he completed S-4. He finished his education at Bishop Comboni College and now lives in Kambuga.

CHAPTER 21

THE BRIDGE IS DOWN

Some people are planners. They will work on a project until everything is just right, all the funding is in place, every piece of paper is reviewed and signed. I am a doer. The minute I realized the board was seriously considering building the secondary school, I got to work. We did not have years to waste. Kutamba would graduate its first class in December of 2012. We could have sixty kids ready to start secondary school the following January.

The five acres I had purchased from my uncle near the Blue Lupin library was along the crest of a hill, but it still needed to be leveled. Even before the feasibility report was finished, I hired a bulldozer to come in and even out part of the land.

When the report arrived in August, it contained a summary of the current situation, projections of land, building and staff costs, funding strategies, project cash flows and a loan amortization schedule. I balked at the thought of taking out a loan. There must be a way to do this without going into debt. We could build as money came in.

School operational expenditures for the first four years if we opened in 2013 would be about $601,812. Private students were expected to generate $458,460 of that, meaning Nyaka would only need $143,352 over the four-year period for the school to break even. We would spend $390,000 to support the same number of students at other schools. Which meant the new secondary school would save us $246,648 over the first four years.

Those figures would make the board happy. It was the other figures that would concern them. The land purchase was already completed. Building expenses were another matter. Classrooms, two dormitories, administration hall, library, workshops, dining hall, main hall, gymnasium, labs and furniture, added up. A $1.6 million cost estimate glared at me from the page.

This was US dollars, not Ugandan shillings. I asked God to step in. It was going to take divine intervention to see this project to the end. He had not let me down so far, but maybe I was taking on more than we could handle.

Somewhat to my surprise, the board did not balk at this but decided we would not start building until we raised half of what we needed. $800,000 was less daunting than $1.6 million, but still a lot of money. I told them I could do it. Fortunately, I was not alone in this commitment. Janis Simon's leadership during this capital campaign and building process was steady, transformational, and unquestionable.

I began to solicit promises from the people who had supported Nyaka in the past. For one million dollars, someone could have their name on the entire school. I did not find any takers. Naming a classroom for $50,000 proved more acceptable. Barry Segal was the first to commit his support of $150,000 for phase one. Janis Simon and Cath Inanir promised $50,000 each to name a classroom. My sisters and family pulled together another pledge of

$50,000. That was $300,000 of what we needed to start.

Sam Ahumuza drew the architectural plans for us. When I received his artist's conception for the school building complex, I could not help but stare. It was breathtaking. The three-story classroom building would be the first multi-story structure in the Nyaka area. White stucco walls supported an orange tiled roof. Arched openings shaded outdoor hallways. Other buildings stood downhill and to the side of the main classrooms. The campus would be a shining example of Nyaka and its educational goals.

"The best is yet to come," I whispered. "With God nothing is impossible." Now, we needed to hire a good contractor.

When I worked at Michigan State University, Maama's back got progressively worse. She needed a modern home with indoor plumbing and solid floors. In 2010 I quit MSU and cashed in my 401K account to build her a house but wanted to make sure I did not end up paying for shoddy construction. I had learned from the mistakes we made with the recently completed library and spoke to Dennis, the engineer who designed the Nyakagyezi water system. He recommended Busy Bee Contracting from Rukungeri, co-owned by Julius Bagiira. Julius was the man who inspected the library and explained that the foundation was cracking because the contractor had not used a moisture barrier.

Julius did an amazing job on my parents' house. When he spotted poor workmanship, he would have part of a wall torn down and rebuilt, or a piece of roofing redone. He was my first choice for the secondary school, and I was pleased when he and his partner, Martin, won the bid.

As impressed as I was by their previous work, I was not sure they were ready for a multi-building project. The school would be a big job. I hired an extra set of eyes to monitor them just in case.

Getting building permits in Uganda can be an arduous process. When we built Nyaka Primary School, we had to travel back and forth to Kanungu Town, the district capital, for permits. Since then the district has been divided into sub-counties. Now there is an official in nearby Kambuga who can carry out inspections and accept paperwork. Julius handled all the permits, and by July 2013, we were ready to erect the first building. I traveled to the village for the groundbreaking ceremony.

People came from all parts of the globe. Kelly Voss, our Director of Development, arrived with a group of women a few days before the event. Becky Schritter, an avid supporter and board member from Sacred Heart Church, came from Farmington, New Mexico. Cath Inanir was there from Turkey and Barbara Kroberger flew in from Philadelphia. Peter Mugisha and other community members, volunteers, grandmothers, students, and local dignitaries arrived the day of the celebration.

Weather is fairly consistent in the village, with cool nights and hot days. July 13th, however, was unusually hot. Instead of having everyone sit outside in the heat, we chose to do the groundbreaking quickly and moved the festivities into the Blue Lupin Library's main hall. A local official gave a speech through the public-address system, but before I was introduced, a man in a dark suit stood up and straightened his suit coat.

"I must interrupt," he said. "This building was not approved by the District. You cannot build here."

The room erupted in groans and complaints. This was typical of government workers. The man wanted a bribe.

"No," someone yelled from the audience. "You cannot do this!"

Another woman stood. "It is not true."

I walked down the aisle. "Who are you?" I asked.

He introduced himself as a district representative.

"It is interesting that the District would wait until this moment to tell us we do not have permission to build." I looked him right in the eye. "Why did you not inform us of this problem before? My contractor has filed all the papers for this construction."

Our foreign visitors looked confused as grannies and local citizens applauded. Several grannies swiveled in their chairs to glare at the man. If they had not been God-fearing women, I am sure they would have cursed him to his face. I imagined them taking up eucalyptus switches and chasing him from the room like a wayward goat.

He stared at his feet, embarrassed.

"This school is being built to benefit this community and the entire district," I said. "It is not for my family. My sons will never attend this school. My parents will not benefit." When I first proposed building Nyaka Primary School, many in the village thought I would run for political office. The school was an attempt to gain their favor. They knew better now. They also knew that I never pay bribes.

"We have guests who have come from afar. Kampala. Europe. The United States. Am I to tell them that they have traveled great distances for no reason?"

People talked among themselves. The man did not answer.

"If you check your office again," I said, "you will find the correct papers have been filed. Do you need anything else?"

Chastised, the man shook his head and worked his way through the crowd to the back door. As the sound of his car starting echoed through the building, applause and cheers filled the room.

"Let us continue," I said. "This is a day to celebrate."

After many speeches, pronouncements, singing, and dancing, a buffet of traditional foods was set out for the guests. Attendees admired the artist's drawing of the new school. There were discussions about the building plans and the students who would attend.

We were never again bothered by the District for permits. When I returned home to Michigan, I wired money to begin construction.

Nyaka Secondary School rose slowly. Wooden scaffolding towered three stories. Bricks, sand, and mortar mix arrived in trucks. Men worked from sunup to sundown, laying bricks one by one.

Although we depend on large donors to support us, smaller donations by church groups, individuals, and children are just as important. Even purchasing our books and granny-crafted products makes a difference. I began several new campaigns to help offset building costs. One was our *Brick by Brick* program. Students in the States were given posters with a drawing of the school. For every fifty cents they brought in, a brick would be colored in. "Did you ever think that YOU could help build a school?" the poster said. "Bring in your 50 cents today to help children across the world in Uganda go to school!"

Fifty cents does not sound like much, but it adds up. Each time I received a colored-in poster, I remembered the workers in the district mixing mud, forming bricks in molds and stacking them in pyramids. They cover the molds with soil and light a fire in the center of the stack to cure the bricks until they harden. Nyaka is like those bricks. Once it is fired, it is a rock that stands the test of time.

Our *Brick by Brick* program was ideal for schools that support

Nyaka. Two such schools are in South Korea: the Korea International School (KIS) and Seoul International School (SIS).

My connection with KIS began in 1998 when I met Kevin Jaramillo in Woodland, California. We were both National CASA (Court-Appointed Special Advocate) volunteers, and since I had no car, we started sharing a ride. It was on one of these rides that I told Kevin I would be building a school for orphans in Uganda. Since he was a teacher, I asked for his advice. He laughed, reached into his pocket, and handed me 36 cents.

"Thank you," I said. "This will buy a few bricks."

"For real?" he said. "You must be kidding."

"I am not. I will consider this your first donation."

We have been friends and brothers since.

Kevin's mom, Emolene, and stepdad, Sam Carpenter, lived in Farmington, New Mexico. He took me to their home and they unofficially "adopted" me. I soon met his sister and his two nephews, Barry Michael, and Taylor. Kevin's brother had passed away, leaving the boys to be raised by their grandparents just like many orphans in my village.

Their church, Sacred Heart Parish, immediately joined our cause. Father Tim Farrell approved a resolution that on every Mother's Day, a second collection would benefit women and orphaned children at Nyaka and Kutamba. For more than ten years, the church has supported us. Father Tim has visited three times with mission teams. Many church members have also visited the schools. One of them later became our treasurer. Becky Schritter visited Nyaka twice and served on the board. She also hosted me and the Nyaka staff when we visited Farmington.

Kevin later accepted a job in Korea and took my book with him. After a Korean-language edition was released, it did not take much to convince the school administration to invite me to speak.

KIS is a premier Pre-K to Grade 12 college preparatory school that offers comprehensive education in humanities, world languages, engineering, arts, math, and science. They also emphasize internationally focused applied learning opportunities. Over the years, their Friends of Nyaka club has hosted various fundraising events, from barbeques to basketball tournaments.

One of the KIS students, Addison Rich, told her parents, Patrick and Danielle, that she wanted to sponsor a child and wear a Nyaka bracelet. Each year, Addie, presented us with a donation envelope filled with her babysitting earnings. Soon, her sister, Sydney, joined the team. Together, they inspired other young people: Willow and Ayla Martin, Sean O'Connor, Lucy and Rubie Lovelin, and many more.

When we began our brick fundraising program, the KIS students were more than enthusiastic. I arrived on my annual visit to find entire walls covered with brick coloring sheets filled with different colors. Teachers had encouraged students to form teams to compete. More than $20,000 was raised by children in Korea. Other countries and schools in Singapore, Brazil, Egypt, UK, Canada, Australia, France, Switzerland, also pitched in.

Many teachers who have heard me speak became involved with our program. When they transfer to other schools, they take Nyaka's message with them. They have "nyakalized" every school they work at. Kevin and his fiancée, Diane, brought Brazil School of Nations on board, Leigh Martin and her daughters found supporters at Singapore American School (SAS), Heather and Chris spread the word to Cairo American School in Egypt, and Hong Kong International School (HKIS) joined our team with

David and Theresa Lovelin's encouragement. I am blessed to have visited each of the schools mentioned above.

Patrick and Danielle Rich became my family in Korea after Kevin and Diane moved on to Venezuela (we cannot wait to "nyakalize" that part of the world!). Patrick and Danielle have since joined the American International School in Abu Dhabi.

Teachers who return to the United States have also "nyakalized" their local schools. Cherry Creek in Denver is now a supporter because of Jeff and Amy Boyce. They took students Abigail Weeks and Lauren McMillen, to Nyaka with solar panels to provide light in the computer room and boys' dormitory.

At least once a week, I called the Kampala office to check on the building's progress. Things moved faster than expected. It was possible the outer walls of the building and the roof would be completed by December when I returned to the village.

It was during one of these calls that the Country Director, Jennifer Nantale, hesitated when I asked her to update our progress.

"There's bad news," she said.

"Oh no." My first thought was that some official was sniffing for money.

"The bridge is out."

"What bridge?"

"The one at the bottom of the Enengo."

"For how long?"

"It's out. Gone. It fell into the river."

Cold water rushed through my veins. A steep gorge separates Kanungu District from the rest of the country. The metal bridge that crossed at the bottom of the Enengo was Kambuga Town's lifeline to Rukungeri District and the rest of Uganda. Everyone used it. Buses transported people from Kampala to western Uganda over it. Trucks hauled cargo to the Congo and Rwanda across it. Tourists crossed it to access Bwindi Forest and its famous mountain gorillas.

"It is gone entirely?"

"Yes, no one can cross. Julius said we have to stop construction."

"They have to get the walls up before the rainy season," I said.

"He said he is concerned about that."

"Then what is the problem? We can get bricks from the local area."

"Kanungu District is out of bricks."

"What?!"

"Julius said they'll have to haul them from Rukungiri. That will cost more."

"How much?" It would be miles and miles extra to drive around the Enengo. That was an extra charge for drivers, trucks, and petrol.

"Probably three times the estimate," Jennifer said.

I did the math. Our donors had pledged over a three-year period in installments. We had just enough to afford the main building this year. There was no extra money for overruns.

"Okay," I said. "I will figure it out. Tell Julius to keep building."

TWINAMASIKO DENIS

Twinamasiko Denis graduated from Nyaka Primay School and went to Ishaka Adventist College before completing Ordinary levels at St. Charles Lwanga.

He then went to Bishop Comboni College in Kambuga for Advanced levels and went on to Ndejje University. He graduated in October 2017 with a Diploma in Social Work and Social Administration. He has two children.

CHAPTER 22

IN NEED OF A ROOF

In January of 2014, Michigan ushered in the usual cold and snow. During winter, many people huddle under a blanket with a good book, but things were different in the Kaguri house. Our home was full of babies. We celebrated Nolan's second birthday. The girls would be one year old in April. Fortunately, we had found a live-in nanny from Uganda to help with chores and babysitting. Tabitha was checking into doctoral programs, including one in Chicago. I was busy with meetings and traveling. There was little time for rest.

At the office, I read through Nyaka's expense report for 2013. It looked good. We had spent 82% of our budget on programming and were supporting 656 orphans and 7,005 grandmothers who cared for approximately 43,000 additional orphans. I was afraid 2014 would not be as positive. Because of cost overruns due to the washed-out bridge, we had run out of money for the secondary school and could not afford a roof to protect the main three-story building.

A missing roof would not have been a problem if the rainy season were not rapidly approaching. Too much water pouring through the building could compromise the structure. I thought of buildings in China that were toppling at that time because their cement mixture contained too much sand. Skyscrapers were crumbling. People had died. We were not going to let that happen to the secondary school.

When we started building, the board promised our donors that we would not take out a mortgage or borrow money, everything would be audited, and the first class would attend for free. My only option was to find someone to donate the emergency money we needed.

Based in Canada, the Stephen Lewis Foundation works with small organizations in Africa, providing care and support for women, orphaned children, grandmothers, and people living with HIV/AIDS. They operate in fifteen African countries and finance sixteen organizations in Uganda. The Nyaka Grandmothers Program has been supported by them since 2007. Since Blue Lupin had pledged money through them for the library construction, I decided to find out if they would advance some additional funds. It could not hurt to ask.

Sarah Layton, the office manager, answered the phone.

"Hi, Sarah," I said. "This is Jackson Kaguri."

"How are you Jackson?"

"I am fine." I was not fine. I was nervous. I did not want to admit we were in trouble. The Nyaka Program had always balanced its budget. "Is Ilana available to speak with me?"

"I'll connect you."

"Thank you." I swallowed. Ilana Landsberg-Lewis is driven and determined. I was glad this was a phone call. I did not think I could handle her intense blue eyes.

"Hello, Jackson. How are you doing?"

"I have a question, uh..." I am not usually tongue-tied but could hardly get the words out. "About funding. The bridge... we have problems with our building costs. The bridge over the Enengo collapsed. Costs are much higher. I am calling to see... can you forward the second installment of your grant early?"

Illana barely paused. "I am so sorry Jackson, but we have our own budget to adhere to."

"I know." I told her about the missing roof and the rainy season. "I prayed you might have something available."

"I am not happy about this, Jackson."

"I know, but we have done good work with our Grandmothers Program. I have never asked for additional money before, and never again."

Ilana went quiet.

"We cannot afford to lose the building," I said.

"I'm sorry, Jackson, but our hands are tied."

"Okay," I managed. "Thank you for taking my call."

I was hesitant to go to our board members. They had been reluctant to start such a big project, and I did not want to upset them. I ended up calling one of our anonymous donors.

"We can't take out a loan," I said. "And we only have a couple of weeks before the rainy season."

"How much do you need?"

"Fifty-thousand dollars."

"That's a lot of money, Jackson."

"I know. I would not ask if it was not an emergency. We will pay you back in three months when we receive the next installment from Steven Lewis Foundation."

"Okay," the donor said. "We'll keep it off the books."

"God bless you," I said.

The donor wired the money to us the next day and the roofing project continued. Trucks carrying orange-painted iron roofing would make the trek from Rukungiri. There were no cranes to lift materials, so sections were carried up the scaffolding by hand to be mounted on the roof trusses.

I still have a photo of the school with the newly completed roof. In the background, the sky is dark with impending rain. I thanked God. We had won the race just in time. The building was saved, and we returned the donor's money in three months as promised.

The opening of my summer newsletter that year was:

> We are so grateful for everything you have done to support your children and grandmothers in Uganda. You are providing 656 HIV/AIDS orphans with free education, two meals every school day, school uniforms, shoes, and everything else they need for success.

It seemed deficient no matter how I worded it. I wanted our supporters to truly understand how much I appreciated them, including the unnamed donors and children who saved their pennies to help. My name was always the one mentioned, but without them, the Nyaka program would not exist. It was still difficult to believe that a two-room school had become a fully functioning primary, then two primary schools, and now, a secondary school *with a roof.* We would admit its first class in February 2015.

I called the Kampala office. Now that we were assured the main building would be completed by the end of the year, we needed to make plans for the 2014 Nyaka and Kutamba graduates.

"*Agandi,*" Jennifer said. She is from Busoga where they speak Lusoga. After working at Nyaka for many years, she has also mastered Rukiga

"*Nigye*," I said. "How are the plans for the graduates coming along?"

"Things are good. I think we'll have about 50 graduates going on to the secondary school."

"And what about the host families?"

Secondary schools in Uganda are boarding schools where students receive housing and food as part of their tuition costs. We had raised $731,600 for the building project but had not been able to build dormitories. Students from Nyaka lived close enough that they would be able to walk home. For the Kutamba graduates, things would not be so easy. Kutamba Primary School was about two hours away by vehicle, and there was no public transportation. They would need sponsoring families in the Nyakagyezi area.

"We're working on that," Jennifer said. "I'm sure we'll find enough sponsors. Some *mukaakas* are willing to take more than one student."

"Good," I said. "I will keep them in my prayers tonight."

MWEBESA IVAN

I am Mwebesa Ivan, 26 years old and single. I recently completed a diploma in civil engineering at Kampala International University. My graduation will be in November 2019. As per now I work on a construction site with my friend Engineer Nelison who is an expert in construction. He is teaching me on managing a site as I search for a job.

My father died when I was young, that is when I was one month. I grew up with my mother and my elder brother in a small village called Kigarama near Nyakagyezi located in Kambuga sub-county.

When I was seven years, one of our relatives decided to take care of my elder brother, he took him to another neighboring sub county where his home is situated. During that time life was hard. I had no school fees and other basic needs because my mother had nothing like any source of income.

A day of luck came when I was seated with my mother at home when a group of people that included Mr. Agaba Innocent, Mrs. Freda the former headteacher at Nyaka Primary School came and told us that they are giving scholarships to orphans who needed help. I was allowed to join Nyaka.

That's the day I got hopes of joining school. I started

schooling and my life changed completely. I started getting things that I never had before from Nyaka.

I settled like any other child with all needs, studied hard completed Primary-7 at Nyaka Primary School in 2008, then joined secondary at Ishaka Adventist college in Busheyi district where I completed Ordinary level. After, I went for advanced level at Mbarara High School, then went to university. All this was possible because of Nyaka foundation. Otherwise I would have never gone to school.

I sincerely thank the executive director of Nyaka foundation, Mr. Twesigye Jackson Kaguri, donors, and all other hands under Nyaka that supported my education and raising up to now.

THANK YOU.

CHAPTER 23

THE BASKET MAN

When I began to travel to Uganda, I brought two suitcases filled to the 52-pound limit with gifts. Sometimes I'd pay for an extra bag, but these days Delta lets me take three bags with my Diamond frequent flyer status. I return to the United States with all three full of baskets made by the *mukaakas* in our Grandmothers Program. Visitors to the school are also asked that they bring two suitcases, one to carry for their personal items and one to bring back baskets. My annual summer trip in 2014 was like all the others. My suitcases rode in the hold, and I leaned back in my seat, preparing to sleep on the flight from Detroit to Amsterdam. As I dozed off, I remembered my own *mukaaka* reading the Bible to me when I was in the hospital recovering from a leg wound that took months to heal. Grannies are the backbone of society. Without them, Nyaka would not survive. We owe them everything.

In Uganda, when parents die, their children are typically adopted by aunts and uncles. However, HIV/AIDS has taken so many lives that an entire generation has been lost. Grandmothers, instead of resting and being cared for in their old age, have taken on the responsibility of raising their grandchildren. In rural areas, most grandmothers are too poor to adequately feed their grandchildren, much less afford to send them to school. Nyaka and Kutamba can only enroll a small number of the thousands who need assistance, so we help other orphans in the district by supporting their *mukaakas*.

Nyaka's Grandmothers Program, under the direction of the Stephen Lewis Foundation, began in 2007. That first year we recruited 4,234 grandmothers to join. These were not just *mukaakas* whose children had died from HIV/AIDS, but any granny who was raising grandchildren.

The grannies form Granny Groups that have an elected leadership chosen from within each individual group. Regional leaders give support and training to several groups. They are also guided by Nyaka staff, but with an emphasis on the grandmothers as decision makers.

The group members determine who among them receives donated items, training, microfinance funds, homes, pit latrines, and smokeless kitchens. This unique model empowers the grandmothers to share their skills, gives them emotional support, and helps them escape poverty. In our first year, we raised enough money to build one new house and seven latrines for the grandmothers most in need.

During every visit to Nyakagyezi, I meet with Ngabirano Godfrey and the team. Godfrey was previously employed with Kanungu District Local Government as an administrative assistant and social worker. He volunteered for us when the Grandmothers Program first began. I was so impressed with his abilities that when we needed a coordinator for the project, we hired him full-time. He is in charge of making home visits, attending group meetings, coordinating granny training, facilitating interventions, and many other activities. The grannies call him *Shwenkuru*, or grandfather.

Byomuhangi Marius was hired as Assistant Coordinator in 2010 and manages the day to day operations in Rukungiri. Agaba Dan is now Assistant Coordinator for Kanungu, and Vian Owamani runs the microfinance loan program.

By 2017, the program consisted of 98 Granny Groups serving 7,301 grandmothers in Kanungu and Rukungiri Districts. Our team members traveled across the mountainous countryside on *boda bodas*. I worried for their safety. During the dry season, the roads are deeply rutted and potholed, and the men have little protection against dust and exhaust fumes. When it rains, the roads are treacherous. Ruts turn into water filled craters. Roadways wash away in sections, leaving only one passable lane. Hours on the road put our team at risk of being killed in a collision. Work trucks and buses travel as fast as possible to make good time. Motorcycles are difficult to see and are often pushed off the road.

As I arrived for our meeting at the library in my rented SUV, I wished we could afford a truck. Our team would not only be safer, but they would have a vehicle for transporting goods to the grandmothers. But that was a dream for another day. The secondary school would need all of our attention and resources for the next few years.

Godfrey met me at the doorway of their office located at the corner of the building.

"*Agandi*, Jackson."

"*Nigye*," I said.

He welcomed me with a firm handshake and invited me inside to sit across from him at a desk covered with paperwork and a computer. He appeared calm and collected, as usual. The cuffs of his dress pants and shoes were dusted with red clay. He had been traveling that morning.

"How was your trip from Kampala?" he asked.

"Long, as usual," I said.

"And how is your family?"

"The kids are growing fast," I said. "Nic will be finishing high school soon. The little ones are full of energy."

Godfrey nodded. "God has blessed us both."

Marius peered in the office door. He is a young man with a round face, a bearded chin and his own determined energy.

"*Agandi*, Director" he said. "Would you like a coffee?"

"Not now," I said. Not only did Nyakagyezi have the only library in the district, the library had its own coffee shop. I turned back to Godfrey.

Marius pulled a chair up to the desk.

"Are you making progress with the granny buildings?" I asked.

"We are on schedule," Godfrey said. "We will complete 15 houses, 25 kitchens, and 25 pit latrines this year."

After the death of their children, many grandmothers have no one to repair or rebuild their homes, kitchens, and latrines. A leaky roof can lead to sleepless nights standing in a corner of their house during the rainy season. Some homes are in such disrepair that grandmothers are afraid of predators attacking in the night. Many do not have a properly built and maintained pit latrine, which can lead to the spread of deadly diseases like cholera. When their kitchens begin to crumble or the roof caves in, grandmothers have only two choices. They can try to cook outside, which is nearly impossible in the rainy season, or they must cook inside their houses. Smoke in poorly ventilated homes is unhealthy.

"We were also able to supply 315 water tanks," Godfrey added.

In 2012, the Michigan, Colorado, Indiana, and Uganda Rotary Clubs joined together to build a gravity-fed, bio-filtered water system at Kutamba school. It supplies over 25,000 people in the region with clean water. But water systems are not economically or logistically feasible for all locations. The best way to help individual grannies is with water collection tanks. They supply clean water to grannies who are far away from water sources or in hilly areas with difficult terrain. Because less time is spent collecting water, food production increases and children have more time for studying. Women and children, relieved of the burden of daily water collection are also less vulnerable to predators.

"All the grannies deserve to have water tanks," I said. "I will find more donors to help them."

"That is my prayer," Godfrey said. "It has been a very successful year, but there is much more to be accomplished."

"I will need complete reports," I said. "And individual stories for our newsletter."

"I was just reviewing the report on Twine Enid," Godfrey said.

"Where does she live?" I asked. Even though he had a computer, Godfrey knows every *mukaaka* by name, and can tell you their history and family situation.

"Kirundwe," he said. That is nearby, part of Kambuga sub-county. "She and her husband care for five grandchildren."

"AIDS orphans?" I asked. I did not recognize Enid as someone who had tried to enroll her grandchildren in Nyaka.

"No," he said. "Three are children of a son who divorced their mother. Two of the children were produced out of wedlock by her daughter."

"Has she been in the program since the beginning?"

"Yes. She joined in 2007 and has been using the microfinance program."

Many grandmothers want to start businesses or are ready to expand the businesses they already own. Unfortunately, they have trouble accessing traditional loans due to their location, lack of credit, and other factors. The Microfinance Program provides credit for income-generating activities to the grannies. This allows the grannies to grow their business, provide for their families, and improve the local economy. Some of our grandmothers buy supplies to make traditional crafts, or raise goats, chickens, or pigs as a source of income.

"What is her business?" I asked.

"Coffee and cows," Godfrey said. "She started with a loan of 300,000 shillings (about $85 US) in 2009. She has taken out loans of 300,000 to 400,000 over the years. One time she bought a young bull with her profits, which she sold a year later for 800,000 shillings."

"She is a keen businesswoman," I said.

Godfrey nodded. "She has been able to afford school fees and scholastic materials for all her grandchildren because of her business success," he said. "Now she plans on training other grandmothers in the group."

The Grandmother Groups had become more successful than I envisioned. They policed their own membership and had no tolerance for idlers. If a granny did not pay her dues or show up to enough meetings, she would be ejected from the group.

"We have another granny in Bikongozo who is a successful tailor," Godfrey said. "She is in Marius' area."

Marius leaned forward on the desk.

"Mugisha Jenifer now calls herself a 'business granny,'" Marius said.

I laughed.

"She is a widow with two teenaged children and a young granddaughter. Jenifer trained in tailoring and received a certificate before her husband's death but didn't have money to start her own business. She has borrowed from her group three times, mostly to buy fabric. Now she has a shop and is training other members of the community for a fee of 70,000 shillings a month. She has made sure that all the children attend school."

"We have many success stories," Godfrey said. "But I have many requests for more latrines and kitchens."

I nodded.

"You need to sell more baskets," Godfrey joked.

"I am selling them as fast as I can," I said. "I suppose you have some for me to take home."

"Oh, yes," Godfrey said. "We have hundreds of baskets for you."

Many of our grandmothers make beautiful woven baskets, bowls, trivets, hats, purses, paper bead jewelry, and other crafts using natural resources and supplies that they purchase with the help of microfinance loans. We buy these crafts from the grandmothers at a fair price and sell them abroad through basket parties, on our Etsy website, or in stores. The profits go right back into the Grandmothers Program.

"I have my usual two suitcases," I said. "Fill them up."

In my village, I am called *Director* because of the Nyaka program. When I am home, I am *Dad*. At Detroit airport customs, I have returned so many times carrying bags of crafts that they call me the Basket Man.

TUMWEBAZE MOREEN

After Nyaka Primary School, Tumwebaze Moreen joined St. Charles Lwanga where she completed Ordinary levels, the first four years of Secondary School.

She then attended Gables Vocational Training Centre, doing hair dressing and salon management as her course.

She is married to a carpenter and owns a small retail shop in Ruhinda, Rukungiri District.

CHAPTER 24

GRAND PLANS

When the secondary school opened in February 2015, the exterior of the building was complete but not all classrooms were finished. That did not dampen the spirits of the fifty-six students who began their Senior-1 year. Kutamba students had been placed with host families and some experienced homesickness for a while, but our teachers and grandmothers were there to help.

I worried about the $900,000 we still needed to complete the campus. Our customary large donors had stepped up to begin the project, but individual donations only went so far. I made an appeal to our supporters worldwide. The secondary school was a boarding school without dormitories. We needed money to build them.

Thankfully, we found a couple in Michigan willing to finance both the girls' and boys' dormitories. They had been involved in the water project for Kutamba school and I did not expect them to be even more generous, but they were moved to participate in our grand project. I wish I could give them credit, but this God-given man and his wife wish to remain anonymous.

We chose to build the girls' dormitory first. The boys would have to sleep in classrooms until we could complete the second building.

While we waited for that construction to complete, we continued to look for additional sources of funding. The Waislitz Global Citizen Award looked promising. Wendy Schneider had received an email asking for nominations and forwarded it to our Development Director, Daniele Reisbig, to research and possibly apply. Barb Dunlop made the official nomination.

Alex Waislitz is from Melbourne, Australia and Executive Chairman and Founder of the Thorney Investment Group. The Global Citizen is a campaigning website where people can learn about many world issues. It partners with and supports organizations around the globe.

Their webpage said they aimed "to unlock the power of every individual to play his or her part in the movement to end extreme poverty in the next 15 years." This coincides with United Nations 18 Sustainable Development Goals. The award is based on merit in four key areas: global citizenship, impact, innovation, and potential.

That is us, I thought.

Organizations are voted for by people across the world. The winner would receive $100,000, but the competition was steep, with nearly 10,000 applicants. Nyaka was undoubtedly small compared to some groups that applied.

I agreed to try. Daniele filled out their questionnaire. At the end she asked me their last question, "Why should we vote for you?"

Because I am desperate, I thought. I did not intend to let the kids down.

"The work that I have been able to do through the Nyaka AIDS

Orphans Project is the most important thing I have ever done," I dictated to Daniele. "Over the last 14 years it has grown into a holistic, human rights-based model for community development." By now our model had been implemented in many communities in Uganda, Kenya, South Sudan, Rwanda, DRC, and other developing countries, but we needed to create systems and a marketing strategy to reach even more places. The award would help us spread word of our impact and aid the NVSS capital campaign. We focused on the children and women we were helping and emphasized our plans for making the project self-sustaining.

"Personally, I am honored to continue to be a voice for the voiceless," Daniele typed, "a vessel in which hope and dignity is restored in the rural villages of Uganda."

We submitted the entry in July before I left for the secondary school's official Grand Opening of the Nyaka Vocational and Secondary School. People would attend from far and wide, including Ronny and Janis Simon.

We landed at Entebbe, took a small plane from Kampala to Kihiihi, and rode to the village in a van rented from BIC Tours, owned by my lifelong friend, Sam Mugisha. Professor Mondo would arrive the next day. Canvas canopies had been set up in the grassy area near the school construction.

Teacher Pius acted as the master of ceremonies. He encouraged the students to dance while guests seated themselves in folding chairs within the canopies' shade. Attendees donned their best clothing even if those clothes were well-worn suits and frayed-hem dresses. This was a celebration.

Nyaka kids sang songs. I gave a speech thanking everyone and encouraging the students to do their best. Comfort and Martina from the secondary school's first class, presented a poem entitled: "I Can't Finish Talking." That was followed by a ribbon-cutting ceremony and classroom dedications.

The first one was dedicated to Janis Simon by her husband and children. The second classroom was dedicated in honor of Teacher Freda Byaburakiirya by board member and long-time supporter, Cath Innir. The third classroom was named in honor of my parents, sisters, their children, and other relatives, who also contributed.

Ronny Simon spoke first, holding back his tears. "When Jackson first approached me and the board about building this school, we all said no. I personally told him there was no way he would be able to do this in his lifetime. I am not a believer, but I can now say there is a God and that God loves Jackson and loves you all. Jackson is my brother and I am honored to be here on behalf of my children and my entire family. It's an honor to serve and save lives in this community. Please know that we are honored to be here."

Professor Mondo urged people to work hard to improve literacy. Guests were presented with handmade gifts from primary, secondary, and vocational students. We served a cake shaped like the school. The kids took delight in eating this rare treat and drinking soda pop. An hour later, the ceremony ended with more music and a prayer. Overall, it was a great day, but the unfinished rooms reminded me that we had a long way to go.

Upon my return to Michigan, I was surprised to find an email from the Waislitz Global Citizen Award competition. We were one of 12 finalists! I could not wait to share the news with Tabitha.

I checked the time. Tabitha had started her doctoral program at Illinois School of Professional Psychology at Argosy University in Chicago. During the week she stayed with Kate Tillery, a friend

Tory Dietel had connected us with. I took the chance she would not be busy.

"Hi, Love," she said.

"Hello. Are you busy?"

"I'm walking to class, but I have some time."

"Then I have time to tell you the good news. We are a finalist for the Waislitz award."

"That's great." The sound of her joy even through the phone's tinny speaker made my skin prickle.

"We need to create a video explaining our project," I said. "They are going to be posted in August and we must get online votes through the Global Citizen website. The one that receives the most votes will win the $100,000 award." By that time, I had been interviewed many times, CNN had produced mini documentaries at the school, and *Time* magazine had filmed me in my house, NPR had interviewed me for the book, and I had done some video blogs. It should not be difficult to produce a snappy pitch.

"We'll get plenty of votes," she said. "The best is yet to come." She apologized for cutting the conversation short, but she had arrived at her building. "Love you."

"Love you too."

NYAKA VOCATIONAL SECONDARY SCHOOL

The Nyaka Vocational Secondary School groundbreaking took place July 2013 and opened on February 9, 2015 to 50 students from Nyaka and Kutamba Primary Schools.

In 2016 The Nyaka Vocational Secondary School educated more than 160 students. Six of eight buildings were operational: the Administration Building, Girls Dormitory, Boys Dormitory, Biology and Computer Labs, and the Carpentry, Brick Laying, Mechanical, and Metal Workshops.

CHAPTER 25

EDJA FOUNDATION

July of 2015 was a busy month for Nyaka. I arrived with Janis Simon, Richard Segal and his daughter Annie, Cath Innir and her niece Katarina, Leah and her daughter Romi, and Nic.

Professor Amy Sarch, Director of Women's Studies at Shenandoah University followed with her teenage daughter, Zoe, and a team from the university. They stayed at the Kigezi Forest Cottages, a local resort built into the cliffside by Sam Renzeho, not far from the school.

I met Amy in 2010 when I became part of her Going Global First Year Seminar program. I was invited back each year to speak to freshman and we became good friends. Every time I visited, I invited her to come to Nyakagyezi to witness what we were doing firsthand. She told me she wanted to, but there was always an excuse why should could not. Finally, I thought of an idea.

"I would love you to do a women's studies class for Nyaka," I said. "I want to empower our girls like you do your freshman at Shenandoah."

"I don't know," she said. "Uganda is an entirely different culture."

"Not as different as you think. Besides, our girls will be going to college and need to understand life beyond the village. We can use your help."

"Maybe I can develop a short program that the university might be interested in funding."

"Good," I said. "I will have Jennifer from our Kampala office send you some material."

The university approved her idea. Amy developed a workbook entitled *You Are Beautiful.* It contains sections on Self-Esteem, Growing and Changing, Avoiding Early Pregnancy, and Saying No, among others. It was just the sort of thing we needed. Plus, it finally got her to visit Nyaka.

After taking some time to adjust, they traveled to Kutamba where Amy spent about four hours going through the workbook with a group of 12- and 13-year-old girls. The first page asked about things such as what they liked and disliked, their favorite food, when they felt happy and sad, what scared them, etc. Other sections prompted them to draw pictures of girls and boys doing expected chores. The last page read, "You are beautiful. Fill this page with pictures and words that tell me why you are beautiful."

Afterward, Amy joined Lydia's class at Nyaka, and I met with Amy and Zoe for dinner at the cottages. Amy seemed satisfied with what they had accomplished but had some reservations.

"The girls were very cooperative," she said. "Honestly, I didn't get to know them very well. But we did do role playing with the 'NO' exercise. They drew pictures of themselves saying 'no,' and pictures of what it means to be beautiful."

"You are unhappy about it?"

"I'm concerned with how the girls answered some questions. In the part that asks them to list three things they don't like, many answered, 'I do not like getting raped.' I'm also alarmed that these girls feel they cannot do boys' work like collecting wood or tending animals because they will get raped. I don't know if this is what they are taught, or if it's something they've experienced."

"Rape is a very real fear," I said.

"But how often is it happening? There are signs posted about abstaining from sex, using condoms, and avoiding HIV, but would a girl report a rape to a teacher?"

I did not know. The justice system in Uganda is not the same as in the United States. If a woman reports rape to the authorities, she must pay to have the accused man transported to jail and brought to trial. Rapists prey on poor girls whose families cannot afford to prosecute. If the family makes a fuss, the rapist might bribe them with a goat or a few chickens.

"I'm particularly concerned about one girl in Lydia's class," Amy said. "Susan. She chose red crayon to write her answer about rape. It was the only time she used the color in her workbook. Lydia said she would talk to her after class."

It turned out that Susan had not had any problems, but Amy's classes made an impact on both the teachers and the students. The girls became more comfortable talking about healthy sex, about their bodies, and creating boundaries. The teachers learned how to recognize and report a girl they thought might have been raped.

During Amy's stay, Tabitha arrived with three women from our church, Pearl Johnson, Valerie Crawford, and Peggy Ogglesby. They had raised money to build a house for a *mukaaka* in the Grandmothers Program. Sometimes people want to do more than donate money. For them, we offer a chance to help build a house, kitchen or latrine from the ground up.

These women joined a local contractor who furnished materials and supervised the construction. They got their hands dirty setting poles and weaving the cross hatching, mixing and applying mud daub, and climbing to the top of the structure to nail the metal roof.

After they finished, they joined me on a trip to Kutamba school. I met with teachers while they toured the buildings. It was that day that I saw firsthand how Amy's course had changed perceptions. A nine-year-old girl named Grace had been raped. The incident, which normally would have been ignored because nothing could be done, was reported.

I searched for Tabitha and found her with the women in the teachers' lounge.

"We have a reported rape," I said.

"One of the students here?"

"A nine-year-old."

"Oh my God." Pain lined Tabitha's face.

"A thirty-five-year-old man raped her last weekend," I said. "Grace's *mukaaka*, Granny Rose, said he had the nerve to offer her a goat. She refused. The police will only arrest him if Granny Rose pays the $12 holding fee." That was equal to half a month's wages.

"Where's Grace now?" Tabitha asked.

"She is here at school." Grace had walked to school that morning despite her trauma. Carrying the burden caused her to retreat into a shell, but she did not miss a day of class. It was not until an alert teacher noticed the change in her demeanor and asked the right question that she broke down in tears and told her story.

Tabitha stood. "I'll talk to her." She met with Grace and the school nurse. That evening at the house, she was still shaken.

I sat beside her on the sofa. "Tell me what you are thinking."

"It feels like my heart is breaking," she said

"Both of our hearts," I said.

"I still feel..." Tears welled in her eyes. "I should be strong and help these girls, but the shame and embarrassment are still with me... from my own experience. I am..."

"You are one of the strongest women I know," I said.

Tabitha wiped her eyes.

"When we first met," I said, "you were determined to help abused girls."

"That's before I had three babies at home and my PhD to finish." She sighed. "I barely have time to get my work done as it is."

I pulled her into my arms. "I do not know if Grace is the first student to experience this, but she is the first to do something powerful. She spoke up."

"I know. I know."

"Before we married, I promised I would support you in every way," I said. "You cannot allow fear to hold you back. Use your voice to help little girls. Demand justice for the victims. I will be at your side no matter what."

Tabitha breathed deep. "I don't know if I can do it."

"God will take care of the important things," I said. "*I* will get the initial paperwork going."

In Michigan we began the process of creating the **EDJA** Foundation. The first part of the name honored Tabitha's mother, Edith, who had dedicated her life to be a voice for the voiceless and standing up for what is right. The other half honored my mother, Janet, who had survived poverty and domestic violence.

Grace became the first girl helped by the new program. She received counseling to guide her healing process, and her attacker was tried and sentenced to ten years in Kanungu prison. Like all prisons in Uganda, Kanungu is overcrowded and in deplorable condition. Prisoners must work on farms to earn food and other necessities like soap, salt and medication. There have been reports of torture as recently as 2017. The man would certainly be punished for his actions.

Now, if we can only prevent the crime from occurring in the first place, EDJA will have done its job.

NIWAKORA FREDIAN

Niwakor Fredian went to Nyaka Primary School for Primary level. After this, she attended Ishaka Adventist College for Ordinary level.

She graduated from Gables Vocational Training Centre with a certificate in tourism and hotel management.

She has worked in several hotels, including Kigezi Forest Cottages. Currently she is married and not working. She has no child yet and is married to the owner of a small shop in Muhakya, near Kambuga.

She thanks the Director, donors, and entire Nyaka family for the assistance that was rendered to her while in School.

CHAPTER 26

GLOBAL CITIZEN

There are plenty of Nyaka supporters around the globe. Thousands of international, university, high school, and middle school students had read *A School for My Village* by the time we competed for the Global Citizen Award. Central Florida had even chosen the book for its 2013 One Book, One Community initiative, prompting the entire freshman class at the University of Florida to read about our work. We had a chance.

I worked with the office staff to put together a video. It had to be catchy and original, something that would grab people's attention. I decided to hold a soccer ball while I spoke. Not just any soccer ball, but one made by one of the village kids out of banana fiber. At the end of the talk I held it forward and said, "The ball is in your hands. Go vote."

We promoted the video among our friends, donors, and followers on Facebook and other media sites. I expected Nyaka votes to pour in from our amazing supporters as soon as the finalists were posted.

My confidence remained high until the evening the Global

Citizen website went live. Once I read books to the kids and tucked them into bed, I settled before the computer in my basement office. The award finalists were posted. I scrolled down through our competitors.

That was when I saw it: water.org.

Oh no.

Later, when I went upstairs to the kitchen, Tabitha saw my face. "What's the matter?"

I sighed. "I was looking at the Global Citizen website. Our video looks good. We should get a lot of votes."

"Then what's wrong?"

I fished an orange from the fruit basket on the counter. "Water.org is one of the organizations."

"Isn't that run by someone famous? An actor?"

"Yes. Matt Damon, of all people. He must have a million fans. Water.org's goal is to bring safe water and sanitation to the world through access to small, affordable loans. It is a great organization with a noble purpose. I do not see how we can get more votes than them."

"Keep your faith," she said. "God hasn't let you down yet."

She was right, of course, but it was hard to believe that Nyaka could compete with Matt Damon. I said extra prayers. *The money is not for me. It is for the kids.*

Late in August after a long day at the office, I checked email one last time before picking Nic up from music practice. A new message from the Global Citizen Foundation was in the queue. I moved the cursor over it but hesitated.

"Please let this be good news," I prayed.

I clicked. The email opened.

"We are pleased to inform you that you are one of four finalists..."

We made it to the final four! I read it again, and then again. They were going to pay for airfare and accommodations in New York for the week of September 18th through September 23rd to attend the 2015 Global Citizen Festival Live, Movement Makers, and the Global Citizen Festival.

"For the winner and a guest," I read aloud. Tabitha could come with me. I looked at my watch. She was in class. I would have to wait until later to call her. I read the email once more to make sure it was real.

When I called Tabitha with the news, she was as excited as I was, but had classes the night the winner would be announced. My heart sank, then rebounded as she added, "I can come in later that night." After confirming her schedule, she booked a flight from Chicago to New York. She would be there in time for the festival.

Two weeks later, I packed my best suit and arrived at the Detroit airport just in time to board the plane. I was overjoyed and nervous at the same time. Barry Segal had offered to let us stay at his apartment in a high-rise building along 56th Street. It was on the opposite side of Central Park from the Guggenheim offices where our meetings would be, but not too far.

When I arrived for our first meeting, I was impressed with the Guggenheim's modern design. The most dominating part of the building is a circular white multi-level structure a bit like a large cup, wider at the top than the base. The inside is just as striking, with a curved atrium surrounded by tiers of walkways.

I found my way upstairs to the Global Citizen Impact Lab. About thirty people gathered there, including several business leaders, a member of last year's winning organization, and of course, Alex Waislitz. Alex shook my hand and greeted me in his Australian accent. He was younger than I expected for someone so financially successful.

I met many influential people that day. One was Scott Minerd, a senior partner with Guggenheim Partners, an intimidating man with wide shoulders and a broad chest. I found out later he was a bodybuilder with many interests.

The others competing for the award were introduced. Daphne Nederhorst, founder of Sawa World, had an ambitious goal of lifting 1.2 billion people out of poverty. Nyla Rodgers was the founder of Mama Hope, a program that focuses on making small, local projects self-sustainable.

The third finalist was represented by Gary White, Matt Damon's co-founder. Despite my competitive urge, I found Gary to be a very interesting, intelligent man. Even if water.org won, this was a networking opportunity for the Nyaka program. I had already won just by being in the presence of these amazing and highly influential people.

Guest speakers suggested numerous ways to improve our organizations. Even though this was good information and I learned more than expected, I kept thinking about the award. With that money we could finish classrooms and complete more buildings.

When the impact Lab was over, we moved to an open reception area, joined by more invited guests. In addition to Alex, Andy Bryant of Segal Family Foundation, Spencer Ton of the Cordes Foundation, and many other wealthy, well-connected friends of the Guggenheim were in attendance.

Finally, the time came for Scott Minerd to announce the winner. He nodded to the finalists. "Now, what we want to hear in sixty seconds or less is who you are, what you're up to, and how you'll change the world."

Daphne went first and I was second. My heart raced so fast I do not even remember what I said. Nyla and Gary spoke after me, but I did not hear what they said, either. This experience was definitely larger than life.

"Let me say," Alex said, "that was all the preamble." He cleared his throat and smiled "This year we had great organizations doing amazing work around the world. But the moment we have been waiting for is here, so the winner, who is around the table... is Jackson."

Jackson? Who is Jackson? I glanced wildly around the room and finally settled on Alex's calm demeanor. Yes, he had said my name. My chest went numb. I moved forward to shake his hand. He gave me a hug. I could not believe it. I wanted to jump up and down and do a traditional dance, but I kept calm and thanked him. The next I knew I was being interviewed on video by a young woman.

"On behalf of all the children," I said, "and on behalf of all the grandmothers who do not even know what voting is, I thank you. This is a huge, huge win for these people."

The interviewer asked if I was ready to appear on stage in front of 60,000 people.

"No, I am not," I admitted. "But I will be when my wife gets here tonight."

I called Tabitha. She had scheduled the flight from Chicago to New York and arrived later that evening. The next day was the festival and the whirlwind continued.

Festivities took place on the Great Lawn in Central Park. A stage had been erected at one end. A huge red half-circle arched over the stage, which was also backed with red curtains. This created a striking presence and echoed the Global Citizen logo of a red globe.

Beyonce , Jay-Z, Ed Sheeran, Coldplay, and Pearl Jam were just a part of the entertainment. Malala, Hugh Jackman, and Leonardo Di Caprio spoke. Other dignitaries, including Vice President Joe Biden and Michelle Obama, also made appearances. Once again, I felt humbled to be in the presence of so many great people, and just two feet from the amazing First Lady. What an honor.

Tabitha and I received an all-inclusive pass to the green rooms. I was surprised to discover that Beyonce had more visible security than Michelle Obama.

When Scott Minerd walked on stage in a suit and an LA Dodgers baseball cap, I felt self-conscious wearing the green and tan African shirt Tabitha had suggested. She squeezed my hand and I glanced at her. She was as beautiful as ever in a short-sleeved African dress colored in oranges and browns, hair styled into long braids. I tried to let that thought comfort me, but my stomach was like a brick.

"On behalf of Guggenheim Partners," Scott said. "I am honored to be standing here in front of an audience of 60,000 people driven to ending extreme poverty, and doing the measurable, meaningful work to bring about the change that is necessary to millions of people around the world. But I'm not here because of Guggenheim Partners. I'm here because of you, because of the work that has gone on because of all of you."

Alex Waislitz stepped forward, eyes shaded by his black Australian hat. It was not warm that day, but my cheeks steamed. Even with Tabitha at my side, this was a bigger event than I had ever participated in. Sixty thousand people. All I could see was an ocean of faces.

"Wow, it sure is a star-studded evening," Alex said, "and it sure is good to see some friends and fellow Aussies like Hugh Jackman here to support the cause. The real stars, of course, are those people at the grassroots level around the world working tirelessly to help bring an end to poverty. I created the Waislitz Global Citizen Award in partnership with the Global Poverty Project to shine a light on their work and to help them do even more. We are inspiring one to inspire many."

My heart hammered so hard I feared it would beat out of my chest.

"Now, after losing a brother and a sister to HIV/AIDS, this year's winner has worked tirelessly for 14 years to help thousands of orphans who have lost their parents to this terrible disease. He has succeeded by building schools, introducing sustainable farming, and empowering mothers and grandmothers. Please welcome the winner of the 2015 Waislitz Global Citizen Award, Tweisgye Jackson Kaguri."

I edged onto the stage to the sound of thunderous applause. Alex shook my hand and gave me a hug. I waved, then bowed with hands together to the crowd. Quietly, I thanked God.

As if the main festival was not celebration enough, we were invited to a reception at the Museum of Modern Art. Unlike the Guggenheim, this museum is a rectangular granite-and-glass building. A three-story white sign hung sideways down its height, reading "MoMA" in black letters.

The minimalist interior is equally as simple, with a 110-foot-high atrium, white pillars, and sculpture garden.

Scott Minerd approached me. "Congratulations. Do you know what you are going to do with the money?"

"I am going to find someone to match it," I said.

He looked a bit surprised.

I explained that we had a secondary school campus to complete. The award money would help, but we had more buildings to finish. I hoped to get the campus done before we graduated our first class.

"Where do you plan to find your matching money?" he asked.

"You can do it, Scott," I said with a big smile. Maybe I was being forward, but I would never know if I did not take the chance.

Scott smiled back, and I knew I had not stepped too far out of line.

"How about this," he said. "I'll send you three questions. If I like the answers, I'll match your award."

"It is a deal," I said, shaking his hand. Just like that, Nyaka had received a pledge of another $100,000, securing a $200,000 investment in one night. This was the first time we had ever raised that kind of money in a single day. Later, in 2018, an anonymous private donor would beat that record by writing a check for $250,000.

We got the matching money from Scott a year later. I guess he liked our answers.

AHABWE OLIVIA

Ahabwe Olivia attended Nyaka Primary School for primary level. After this she attended Ishaka Adventist College for Ordinary level of secondary school.

She went to Bishop Comboni College-Kambuga for advanced level and then enrolled in Uganda Christian University. She did a Bachelor of Business Administration and specialized in Accounting.

She graduated in November 2018 and lives in Kampala.

CHAPTER 27

ALL THINGS THROUGH CHRIST

In July of 2017, I met the Northern family at Detroit Metro Airport. They had been wanting to visit Nyaka ever since their daughter, Cameron, started raising money for the kids some ten years earlier. We were joined by my good friend Susan Linville and climate change activist, Rhonny Dam, from Pennsylvania.

I am always impressed by the power of friendship. Otto Ray, my good friend from the Bloomington Indiana Rotary Club, introduced me to Bill Humphrey, his childhood friend, who in turn brought Nyaka to the attention of Pastor Ken Snyder of the First Methodist Church in Martinsville, Indiana. Ken was impressed by our organization and invited me to preach and speak about Nyaka. That connection would lead to an even more special friendship.

After my sermon one day, a cute blonde-haired girl with new front teeth approached, pulling her mom behind her.

"Hello," I said. "What is your name?"

"Cameron Northern," she said. Cameron was only seven years old, but her expression was very serious. "I've been praying for two things. The USA troops and the Nyaka kids."

"She has been very concerned for the kids since Pastor Snyder told us you were coming," her mom said.

I thanked Cameron for her prayers on behalf of the children and encouraged her to help in any way she could. I expected that she, like many school children, would save some change to donate to us. That was the year she showed up at the Bloomington banquet with a jar holding more than $800 in change and bills. The jar was so heavy that Nic, six years old at the time, had to help her carry it to the front of the room.

If you ask Cameron what her passions are today, she would say playing soccer, being outside, being with her family and friends, going to church, watching sunsets, and just relaxing and reading a book. She credits her parents with her sense of confidence and her devotion to Christianity. Her life verse is *Philippians 4:13—I can do all things through Christ who gives me strength.* But she also has an undying love for her brothers and sisters at Nyaka and Kutamba schools.

Since that first meeting, she and her parents, Seth and Ali, and her little brother, Brett, have continued to support Nyaka in amazing ways.

"She has no problem asking people for money," Seth has told me. "She has such a passion to help and serve others."

In 2008, Cameron held a school drive and collected 250 pounds of supplies. The following year, she created homemade flower-pens with duct tape and raised $750.

"I like doing different things," she said. "I like to be creative. I'm just really excited to do this."

In 2014, she was a lanky teenager with braces. That year she wrote a letter asking her friends and family to sponsor her for an indoor Triathlon that included swimming a quarter mile, biking ten miles, and running a 5K. On March 28th she completed the event, raising $2,603 for Nyaka.

"This is Cameron's project," Ali told me when they presented the check. "Seth and I are just here to support her."

The next year she responded to an email from us with a picture of our 30 new Nursery Class students. All needed sponsors.

"God has laid His hand on my heart," Cameron said. "I'm going to find sponsors for all the kids." This was a very ambitious goal for a teen, but I had seen what she was capable of, and encouraged her to do it.

Cameron printed a t-shirt with photos of the new students on the back. She wore it everywhere, shared the Nyaka story, and asked people to sponsor a child. Six short weeks later, she called me.

"I wrote letters and talked to everyone!" Cameron said. "I thought it would take all year, but I have the money now." She had raised $13,525 to sponsor the entire class for a year. Cameron became our Super Hero #1.

In 2016, we spoke about her next event.

"I prayed about what would be a good fundraiser," she said. "I think I have a good idea. Instead of taking on something huge, I thought I could do a little every day. That money would add up and I might raise a lot."

"That sounds wonderful," I said. So far, everything she planned succeeded. I was willing to support anything she suggested.

"I decided to take the last 100 days of the year," she said, "to see if I can raise $100 every day. I'll call the campaign $100 for 100. I know it's a big goal, but I have a big God who loves these orphans and wants to see them cared for."

One hundred dollars every day? *Oh my*, I thought. *This girl is unstoppable.*

She made another t-shirt. The front said "100 for 100. Nyaka AIDS Orphans Project." She posted a video on Facebook, wrote letters to friends and family, used social media, and spoke at her school, several churches and youth groups. Some days she raised more than $100 and other days she did not get anything. In the end, it added up to $13,560, more than $100 a day. People gave in honor of birthdays, loved ones, anniversaries, or just because she asked, and she is not shy about asking.

"These are my brothers and sisters," she told me during that campaign.

I glanced across the aisle to where Cameron leafed through a magazine in her airplane seat. I was so glad that she and her family would finally meet the children they meant so much to.

When the flight landed in Amsterdam, we had a couple hours to rest at the airport. Although I have no problem sleeping on planes, I think the others were too excited to get much rest. Everyone looked tired, but we still had eight-hours of travel ahead.

After a short stop in Rwanda to drop off passengers, we arrived at Entebbe airport. It was night by then, and we spent another half hour going through customs and picking up luggage. Sam Mugisha met us at the gate and transferred our bags into the vans. It was almost midnight when we reached the Africana Hotel in Kampala.

The next morning, after a buffet breakfast of traditional Ugandan foods, vans arrived to transport us to the village. On a good day, the journey takes about eight hours. We stopped along the way to take pictures at the equator, and to have coffee and lunch. Susan suggested we visit Mburo Lake National Park to see zebras and the newly introduced giraffes.

We stopped for dinner at a restaurant in Mbarbara. Ugandan service is notoriously slow, so we were probably there for two hours. By the time we drove through Rukungiri and crossed the new cement bridge over the Enengo Gorge, it was dark. Fortunately, the electric lines that now serve part of our district were working and the driveway to my parents' house was well lit.

"We are here," I said. Dozing passengers roused themselves and started to collect their things. The drivers helped us with the bags. After meeting some of my family, the household staff, and our volunteer photographer, Matt Stauble, everyone decided it was time for sleep. I showed the guests to their rooms.

The next morning, the Northerns were anxious to visit the school. They had candy and gifts on hand. Brett had brought a couple soccer balls and wanted to try out the students' skills. Susan and Rhonny looked forward to meeting everyone and guest teaching the older students.

The moment we walked through the gate, word spread that the *bazungu* were here. Kids poured from the classrooms. The visitors were surrounded by a sea of purple uniforms. Each student wanted to give them a hug.

Cameron's eyes filled with tears. After all these years she was able to meet Rebecca, the girl she had sponsored for many years, and the other brothers and sisters she had loved for so long.

"They were so happy to see us," she said afterward. "They know that we are supporting them. They just want to show us their love."

The school's opening assembly included announcements, songs, Bible verses, and morning prayers. Children and staff welcomed their guests. Seth and Ali could not hold back their tears when they were asked to greet the students.

There was not a moment that day that Cameron's hand was not being held or arms wrapped around her. Children asked if she knew their sponsors in the United States. They asked if she could tell them hello and thank you.

As we often do with guests, Cameron and her family were offered a chance to teach classes. The children are always excited to learn from a new perspective. Brett played soccer with the boys. When Cameron joined in, the boys were shocked by her skill. Most girls in Uganda play netball, a game that resembles basketball.

"I was really impressed," Cameron said at dinner. "The kids are really smart. They have great teachers." I began to wonder if she would want to return home. She went on to rave about her encounters with Rebecca, her sponsored child.

The boy that Brett supported was a Kutamba student. Brett was so anxious to meet him that I had the van go pick Darius up and bring him to Nyaka. They spent the rest of the evening talking and playing video games on Brett's phone.

We continued to Kutamba the next day. Cameron and her family witnessed the poverty that exists in the district. Toddlers wandered near the roads with little or no clothing, often playing in the dirt. Older children helped their mothers dig in the fields or carry kindling on their heads. Many young boys tended goats and cows.

"They should be in school," Cameron said.

"They can't afford books or supplies," Matt told her.

When children saw the van was transporting white people, they ran to the road shouting, "*Muzungu! Muzungu!*" Cameron and Brett waved to everyone.

"It's really sad," Cameron said. "They really don't have a future. Our Nyaka orphans are so fortunate to have us."

Kutamba students and staff welcomed the visitors with songs. Susan and Rhonny taught the older students about immunity, infectious diseases, climate change and the environment while the Northerns worked with younger students. During Rhonny's question and answer time, the conversation turned to birth control and family planning.

The next day, the guests toured the Blue Lupin Library and met Shillah and Ronald who were volunteering in the coffee shop. These two Nyaka graduates were on break while waiting for their national exam results, which would determine if they would attend a university. Generally, Ugandans do not drink much coffee, especially people in the village who grow their own coffee beans. It is the *muzungu* guests who generally take advantage of our library café.

As Shillah made drinks, Ronald chatted.

"We are so happy you have come to visit us," he said. "We are thankful for your support. Our education means everything to us."

Cameron beamed. "I have a new sister and brother in Uganda."

I had scheduled several meetings but tried to spend time with guests in the evening. One day they visited Queen Elizabeth National Park and reported being most impressed by the elephants and hippos. Another day they attended a meeting of the Bwindi Grandmothers Program and stopped in on other *mukaakas* having houses, kitchens, and latrines built. They brought bags of corn flour, beans and rice as gifts.

"I'm amazed at how far our money can go here," Cameron said. "Now I see how a couple dollars a day can change a life forever."

I nodded. I think Cameron always knew this intellectually, but now she understood it in her heart. She had made a bigger impact on the kids and their families than she would ever know.

Because we appreciated Cameron's generous spirit, and because her sixteenth birthday happened to occur during her visit, we spent several days planning a surprise Sweet Sixteen birthday party. She was shocked when she returned from a day's journey to find canopies pitched in the front yard. My sister Faida's catering company had prepared roasted goat and lots of traditional foods.

Birthdays are not traditionally celebrated in the village and if they are, cake is never made. Since Nyaka School's grand opening, however, cake has become an accepted practice. Faida made a birthday cake with flaming fireworks candles. It was quite a wondrous spectacle.

Teachers, guests, and Cameron's sponsored class gathered at one table. Cameron was seated at the head of the guest of honor table beneath the other canopy. She looked both pleased and embarrassed.

The kids sang and danced. "When Jesus say yes, nobody can say no, I know who I am by...."

Speeches were given and food served from a buffet table. As the evening wore on, recorded dance music from the PA system filled the night air.

As Cameron graciously thanked everyone for their kindness, I could not help but smile. The little blond-haired girl I met ten years before was growing into a generous woman with the power to transform the world. I could not wait to see what she would accomplish next.

BAREKYE ONESMUS

Barekye Onesmus graduated from Nyaka Primary School. He attended Ishaka Adventist Secondary School until S-2 before dropping out.

He lives in Kampala working as a hair stylist specializing in color.

CHAPTER 28

BLESSED WITH FAMILY

Being the Director, as the Nyaka kids call me, is a blessing. I have witnessed the construction of two primary schools, library, farm and clinic. I watched our secondary school bloom into existence. One success has followed another. Hundreds of students will have better lives because of their free education, thousands more benefit from the program.

When we published our 2017 report the numbers were staggering even to me. More than 450 students were attending Nyaka and Kutamba schools, 54 percent of them girls. A hundred students had graduated primary, secondary, vocational, high school or university. We served more than 300,000 meals, evaluated more than 11,000 people at the clinic, served more than 3,000 patrons at the library, and offered computer training classes to nearly 200 people.

Almost half of our Pioneer Students attended university. One, Niwabiine Hillary, is now in medical school. Two students, Sarah Riunkado and Bonita Amanya, joined the Nyaka Pioneers at Secondary Level and received full scholarships.

Our technovators, a group of secondary school students pioneered by Comfort, Primah, Uditah, Ruth, Shamim, Maritina and Immaculate, have built robots, created phone Apps, designed security systems, and received national recognition. They pitched some of their ideas at the 2017 National Pitch Even in Kampala and won the Best Live Pitch.

Maritina was one of 100 girls selected from seven nations to attend the WiSci Girls STEAM Camp in Malawi, sponsored by the U.S. Department of State's Office of Global Partnerships, Girl Up and World Learning. Since then, the group has added Brea, Anthony, Michael and Dorothy. I see nothing but success for these innovative students.

Our Grandmothers Program helped over 7,000 grandmothers climb out of poverty along with an estimated 43,000 grandchildren. To date, we have built 283 houses, 613 pit latrines, and 479 kitchens for our grannies. We have furnished 315 water tanks, trained 2,260 grannies in sustainable farming techniques, and made $142,000 in micro-loans, $60 at a time. I could not be prouder of what we have accomplished as an organization.

As much as I love my Nyaka family, being the Director is also a burden. I have spent countless hundreds of hours driving and flying, attending fundraisers, meeting students across the United States and the globe, speaking before the United Nations, accepting national and international awards. All that travel takes me away from my own family. In the years since Nyaka's inception, Nic has become a fine young man in the blink of an eye. Nolan and the twins have started school.

In 2018, I decided a holiday with Tabitha and the kids was paramount. The last time the little ones visited the village was 2013 when they were babies. I wanted them to know their grandparents, aunts, uncles and cousins. Tabitha had family in Rwanda that she had not seen in years. And I longed to spend time in my home village, not as fundraiser, educator or Director, but as Twesigye Jackson.

We made plans to spend the entire month of July in Uganda and Rwanda. Nolan and the girls have jars in their room for saving and spending money. They set money aside for the trip and grew more and more excited as the time approached.

On the day of the flight, Nic, now sixteen, took everything in stride. He had flown many times. The little ones could not wait. They each had their own backpack, their own seat and their own boarding pass. They were little grown-ups until the endless flight took its toll. By the time we reached Uganda, my little grown-ups were grumpy and sleepy kids.

We stayed at Sam Mugisha's house the first night. The next morning, we woke to a bright, sunny day and a breakfast of fresh bananas and pineapple. Sam had three girls, aged nine, six, and three. They were so excited to have company, he let them skip school that day.

The trek to the village was a day of a thousand questions. Why is that girl walking with sticks on her head? Who are those kids in the brown uniforms? Are they Nyaka students? What are those goats doing next to the road? Who is that man on the motorcycle? Why is it so dusty?

When we reached the equator, they had fun standing with a foot in each hemisphere. A man showed them how water circles in opposite directions on each side. Just outside of Mbabara, they noticed the long-horned cattle. Are those real cows? Will they charge at us?

Maama was waiting in her wheelchair when we pulled through the gate onto their property.

"There is your *mukaaka*," I said. "She has been waiting all day for you to get here. Go give her a hug and a kiss." The vehicle door opened before I had time to put it into park. Nolan led the charge, running on loose stones. Tessa followed, and Talia, who is a bit shy, came behind. Maama gathered them in her arms just as she had held me when I was a boy, crying with a scraped knee or stone puncture in my foot. She spoke to them in Rukiga and was surprised when they answered in kind.

Maama and my kids bonded immediately. Since she spent much of her day lying on a floor mat due to her bad back, they visited her each morning and prayed with her. Throughout the day, they brought books and coloring pages to show her. Maama glowed with all the attention and affection.

Taata visited each morning, once bringing fresh-laid eggs and other times announcing milk was ready. One day Talia thought the eggs were hard boiled. We ended up with yolk all over the table.

Not once did Taata grow impatient with the kids or raise his voice, not even when they decided to chase chickens around the yard. Was this the same man who raised me? Something had mellowed in him. The anger that caused him to abuse us verbally and physically seemed to be gone.

Our first day at Nyaka school was overwhelming. Everyone had heard about the twins and kept asking about them. How are the twins? When are they coming? When we walked through the gate, hundreds of students came running. Nolan and Tessa basked in the attention, but it was too much for Talia. That evening she said, "I don't want them running again."

The Nyaka students were overjoyed to have my kids join them in class. Nic helped with the older students. The tailor had made uniforms for Nolan, Tessa, and Talia. They loved them so much, they did not want to take them off.

Nolan joined the Primary-1 class and spent most of his free time on the basketball court. After sitting for years, we had finally been able to have the cement repaired, the court painted, and nets installed.

Overall, the kids settled right into village routine. It did not take the girls long to feel at home in pre-school, Tessa made three friends immediately. They loved new foods like jackfruit, little bananas, and passion fruits. Fanta was immediately popular because we never buy soda pop in Michigan. I had to limit them to one per day. We only watch movies on TV at home, so it was a treat to visit Mukaaka, who kept the TV on all the time for company. They enjoyed having their own bedrooms. The only thing they missed was air-conditioning in cars.

Days flew by quickly. Nic took a spin on a boda boda. Tessa wanted to ride too, so the headmaster took her for a drive. We played local games, like rolling a tire with a stick, and I showed the kids how to cut and eat sugar cane. The little ones were too small to walk to the bottom of the Enengo, but we did hike along the upper edge. Later, Nic and I took the trail to the bottom and crossed a bridge made from a single log over the river.

One day was set aside to visit Queen Elizabeth National Park. We were lucky enough to see elephants close-up. There were also hippos sleeping along the shore, and thousands of birds. We attended three weddings, one for my niece, and two in Rwanda for Tabitha's family. Nic brought his violin and played Amazing Grace at one Saturday church service.

EDJA had won $50,000 from the Waislitz Global Citizen Award just before we left for Uganda. As a result, Tabitha was able to initiate her educational campaign in Kambuga during our trip. It began with meetings and ended in a parade to bring the topic of gender-based violence to the forefront. *EDJA: Victims to Victors*, read the lead banner. A marching band with snare drums, trumpets and tubas led the crowd. Over 1,000 people attended: police, doctors, construction workers, students from Nyaka and many of the surrounding schools, grannies, and visitors.

Matt Stauble filmed the event, capturing school uniforms of every color as the students marched past. A drone flew overhead, recording from above. Each school had created its own sign against violence. Grannies in purple Nyaka dresses sang and danced as they passed. Workers in hard hats participated alongside servers from Faida's catering company in their orange vests. The most encouraging sight for me was a police section carrying a sign: *Police Against Gender Based Violence.*

The parade started at Comboni School playground and ended at the Kambuga market. White canopies had been set up to provide shade, but the crowd was so large only half were able to be seated there. Dancing and speeches followed.

Tabitha took the stage wearing her EDJA t-shirt and ME TOO hat. The crowd listened intently. I could feel the support and power they projected. This would be a changing time for women and girls in the area. I was so proud of Tabitha, I had to blink back the tears in my eyes.

AHARIZIRA BRENDAH

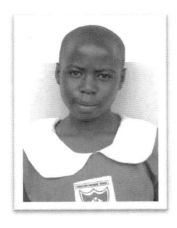

Aharizira Brendah went to Nyaka Primary School for Primary level. After this, she attended Ishaka Adventist College for Ordinary levels.

For Advanced levels, she attended Bishop Comboni College in Kambuga. She then attended Makerere University, achieving a Bachelor of Arts in Education.

She graduated in January 2019 and lives in Kampala, where she works at the Convention Center.

CHAPTER 29

STANDING ABOVE THE WORLD –

CAMP BLESSING

Near the end of our vacation, we went camping with the students. Our annual student camping trips are always a time of drawing closer to each other. This time my entire family was with me.

Taata and I have never spent father-son time together. He practiced fatherhood like an authoritarian dictatorship. *Do as I say. Obey my wishes. Do not talk back.* By the time I was a teenager, we were at odds most days.

Today I realize my father was from a different generation. He had no biological father or good role model growing up. His father died when his mother was pregnant with him. She married another man who resented the two sons that were not his own. My father never felt like a man. When he married Maama, an older woman from a wealthy family, he lived his life trying to prove his manhood with beatings, verbal abuse, and dictating his way.

I promised myself I would never be like my father with my own children. I would always hug Nic and tell him and show him how much I love him. I made sure we spent quality time together. When he was only two weeks old, clearly not old enough to appreciate nature hikes and roughing it in the woods, we took our first trek together in McCormick's Creek State Park near Spencer, Indiana. By the time he was a teen, we had visited many Michigan parks. We hiked through forests and across hills, forded streams, chased snakes, and sat around the campfire, talking and laughing into the wee hours of the morning. It is a time we both cherish.

A great distance separates me from the Nyaka and Kutamba students, but I feel that each of them is my child, too. Because camping is such a bonding experience, I wanted to share that with them, especially since this year the members of Nyaka's pioneer class were readying to start their studies at colleges and universities. My visit in July would be a perfect time to take them on a camping trip.

I made plans months ahead of time. I had recently purchased land in the southeastern corner of Kanungu District to grow timber-producing trees as an investment for college funds. Located on a high ridge, the land looks over a valley where the earth lays like a rumpled blanket. Hills spread across the landscape as far as the eye can see. It is the perfect place to camp.

In the spring, I was invited to Dallas for what had become an annual Nyaka gathering sponsored by Sandra Washburn. I met Sandra in 2011. She had read my book and wanted me to speak to a group of friends interested in knowing more. I soon discovered that Sandra had worked in Northern Uganda and was a founder of a non-profit, called Oysters and Pearls. They integrate technology and science in schools to teach the blind, advocate for women and girls in education and sports, and support wildlife education. They also partner with St. Jude's Orphanage and Consolation Home in Gulu, Northern Uganda. Sandra and I shared a bond of educating the less fortunate.

In Dallas, I mentioned I was thinking about taking the students camping.

"REI Co-op has all kinds of camping gear," she said. Sandra is an extremely determined woman. When she sets her mind to something, it gets done. "Let's look at tents."

The store overflowed with hiking, cycling, and camping gear. I spotted a display of six-person green and white domed tents.

"We need something like this," I said. "Six should be enough." There were only 16 students in the pioneer class, but future class sizes would be closer to 30, not including adult chaperones.

"A good choice," she said. She waved down a worker and we were soon rolling through the checkout.

Purchasing tents was the easy part. Getting them to Uganda was more difficult. We usually transport things in people's luggage to avoid high shipping costs. How was I going to find someone to take tents in their suitcases?

Fortunately, Debi Lang's film crew was on their way to the village and agreed to transport them. I met Debi Lang through an event at Sandra's house in 2014. A director and producer for Caring for the World Films, she began as a TV photojournalist interested in humanitarian causes. When I met her, she had already received recognition for two documentaries: *Hearts of the Himalayas* and *Bittersweet.* When Debi heard the Nyaka story, she asked if we were interested in having our story told. Could she make a film about our program? Of course, I said yes.

With the tents taken care of, I called Jennifer in the Kampala office to set up the excursion and let the pioneer class know we were going camping. When I arrived at the library a few weeks later, the meeting room buzzed with excitement. It was difficult to believe that all these kids would be in college soon. Was it not just yesterday that they started school in their purple uniforms, eyes wide with curiosity and expectation?

"Hello, everybody," I said.

"Hello, Dad."

"Welcome, Director."

The room quieted.

"Tomorrow we are going on a camping adventure," I said.

"What is camping?" Onesmus asked.

"Good question. We are going to drive to some land I own in Murumba. We will hike in the mountains. We will eat goat meat and *matooke* roasted on the fire, have soda to drink, and sleep in tents overnight."

"Tents?" Irene asked. "What if it rains?"

I should have expected that question. The Nyaka program helped build houses for grannies, some of whose only shelters were tents made from blankets and plastic. In a region where people struggled to have a roof over their head, purposefully going into the forest and sleeping in a tent would seem strange.

"The purpose of camping is to get closer to the land and closer to each other," I said. "It is a bonding experience."

"Will we be sleeping on the soil?" Moreen asked.

"The tents are made of nylon," I said. "They have a floor, but the ground will be hard underneath. You will need a blanket. You can bring a mat, but no mattress please."

I explained there would be one latrine but no shower. "We will be hiking part of the time," I said. "I expect the ground to be muddy in places, so wear your older shoes. And wear shorts because you will get hot while hiking. And bring a change of clothing and some deodorant."

"What is deodorant?" Ronald asked. The boys, especially, would stink like *ente* after a day of walking in the hills. Puberty was associated with that smell, and they knew nothing about something called deodorant or how it worked. I certainly did not know when I was their age, either.

"I will bring some," I said. "We will meet here tomorrow."

The next morning everyone arrived early. Hillary, who was being sponsored by Father Tim, a friend from Farmington, New Mexico, was the only one with hiking boots and a rain poncho. Despite my request to wear shorts, the girls came in dresses and good shoes. Because they all played netball, I expected them to have at least one pair of shorts. I was wrong. I went back to my parents' house and found eight pairs of old running shorts with elastic waistbands to loan to them. Come to think of it, I never got those back!

The final count for our trip was sixteen students, Tabitha and my niece, Jolly, Jan Kohler (Debi Lang's cinematographer, who volunteered to help with the boys), and a few drivers and helpers. There was not enough room in the school van for everyone, so we used my sister, Faida's SUV to transport the adults, food, and equipment.

We first traveled to Kanungu Town, where the district offices are located. There, we stopped to purchase bottled water, soda and beer at a small shop. The beer was a gift to appease neighboring adults who would no doubt be curious about our presence on the forest land.

Our students had been to Kanungu Town for parades but had never seen the southern part of the country that borders Rwanda. From town, the road winds up into the mountains, climbing from an elevation of about 4,500 to 7,200 feet. The area we traveled had long ago been cleared and turned into farms.

To the west, the old jungle is protected in Bwindi Impenetrable Forest, home to some of the last remaining Mountain Gorillas. Sam Mugisha, an orphan long before the school opened, runs an international travel agency that brings tourists to see not only the gorillas but the wildlife at Queen Elizabeth National Park. Sam is a prime example of what can be accomplished in Kanungu District. I see Kambuga becoming a small tourist town, welcoming people from around the globe. It will be our students who welcome them.

The road ended well short of the campsite. We parked near a pair of eucalyptus trees, and the students exited the van. I opened the SUV hatch.

"Everyone come take something," I said. "We are walking to the camp."

An old man in a ragged suit, hat, and no shoes arrived, curious about why we were there. I introduced myself as the landowner and told him we were staying for the night. He came along. As we walked the rugged dirt path, several women and teenagers also joined us.

Denis slowed to walk beside me and Tabitha. "How far does your land go, Dad?"

"It is about 200 acres," I said. "It goes very far."

"Are these fields ours?"

"Our land is ahead," I said. "There are pines planted there. We will also plant Eucalyptus trees. In ten years, there will be

80,000 trees to cut for scaffolding, firewood, and electric poles. It is an investment."

Denis nodded and walked ahead to share his newfound knowledge. Tabitha squeezed my hand.

The path followed the contour of the land, growing more and more narrow. Some boys walked ahead, talking and laughing, carrying mats and tents on their broad shoulders. The girls traveled in a group, backpacks and bags stacked atop their heads. Young kids who should have been in school tended a dozen cattle on a steep slope below the path. If not for Nyaka, our kids would be doing the same.

"I am so happy to be here camping," Ronald Arihihi said as he joined us. I noticed he was not carrying anything.

"Where is your bag?"

"Men do not carry bags," he said with a grin. "A woman is carrying it for me." He waved his hands in the air.

"A woman?" Tabitha said.

He motioned behind us. One of the girls carried his bag on her head. "Women love it, Madam," he said. "They love to do that for me."

Tabitha frowned. Even with their education, our students continued to be held back by gender disparity and social norms that favored men over women. These were things we needed to work on and one more reason the secondary school was so necessary.

"Go get your bag," I said. "It is for you to carry."

Ronald looked disappointed. "Okay, Dad."

I had hired workers to level the hilltop and plant grass so we could pitch our tents on even ground. They had also created a fire pit with logs to sit on around the perimeter.

The students dropped their bags and gazed over the valley. Hills covered with a patchwork of gardens and terraced fields rose from the floor. A few trees and houses dotted the landscape. White smoke wound up into the blue sky.

"Oh my God," Hillary said. "I did not know anything like this existed in our country."

"It is beautiful up here," Jan said.

"We are at the top of the world," Denis added.

"Almost," I said. The Rwenzori mountains rose even higher in the northwestern part of the country. They were covered with snow. I thought about taking the students there someday. They would be amazed by the touch and feel of the frozen stuff.

Our first order of business was to assemble the tents. It did not take long for the students to figure out how to stake them and insert the poles. The girls claimed one tent and the boys two others. I pitched mine between them.

Helpers brought in wood and built a bonfire to cook over while we hiked downslope to a spring and up another hill. I gave each student a notebook journal with questions to answer. *Who is one person who has inspired you? Tell me about your life. What are your future plans? If you had one country to live in, which would you chose and why?* We stopped beneath a grove of trees and sat on the needle-covered ground, surrounded by the scent of pine. I gave the students time to write in their journals and talk among themselves.

When we returned, we performed a trust-building exercise. Two students stood behind a third and had to catch them as they fell backward. Some were more trusting than others. A couple girls shrieked as they fell. The experiment ended with much laughter.

Once the campfire was hot, we wrapped *matooke* in banana

leaves to be steamed. Goat meat was skewered on wooden stakes over the coals. By the time the food was ready, almost twenty neighbors sat in the nearby grass. I was not sure we had bought enough beer to make them all happy, but fortunately, we had plenty of meat.

A few years before, the staff had played a joke on me. Library personnel gifted me with a female *embuzi* with three kids. The secondary school staff and the grannies also gave me goats with multiple kids. Goats are traditionally slaughtered for celebrations or given as appreciation gifts. The Nyaka program had helped everyone in the village. They were thanking me for their abundance, but this was way too much.

"What are we going to do with all these goats?" I said. The staff only giggled and smiled. What *was* the Director, who lived far away, going to do with all these goats? Eventually, we constructed a special pen to collect goat manure, and today we have more than eighty goats and plenty of fertilizer for our gardens.

After the meal, I told the neighbors they must go home. I wanted this to be a special time of bonding for the students.

We sat around the campfire talking about future goals and what the students wanted to do with their lives. That was followed by roasted corn for dessert. The girls joined Tabitha in their tent to talk about personal fears and concerns over going off to university. We had brought two tents for them, but they all wanted to stay together for the night.

The boys sat with Jan and me, making jokes and teasing each other.

"The lions will be out tonight," tall Denis said. "That thin tent will not stop them."

"The lion will take the tallest with the most bones first," Hillary said.

"No," Denis countered, "the lion will go for the one with the most meat."

We had serious discussions amid the joking. The boys were concerned about what would be expected of them at university. Having Jan there was helpful, because he was closer to their age and they accepted his advice as they would from an uncle or older brother. I told them about living in the big city, how they would be expected to take care of themselves, and the problems that could arise. I spoke about interacting with girls and warned them of older women who prey on young men by offering gifts, just as older men did with girls.

"I do not know what a condom is, Dad," one of the boys admitted. After all the talk of HIV/AIDS, they were still not educated in important ways.

"I know what a condom is," tall Denis said. "I can show you."

I was not sure if that was a good sign or bad. We did not want the students to be sexually active, but if they were, we certainly wanted them to protect themselves and their partners.

As the sun set, casting long shadows across the valley, peace flowed over me.

"Thank you, God," I prayed. "I have all I have ever wanted in life and can ask for no more."

I thought of all the supporters who had been so generous to Nyaka, the students saving their pennies, the schools in Korea holding fundraisers, little Cameron becoming a force unto herself. People around the world cared. Ugandans, Americans, Canadians, Australians, English, Europeans, and Asians, all added what they could to support the Nyaka project.

Roasted goat meat and corn on the cob was added to the coals to warm. Blue sky gave way to blackness. Stars spread across the sky, brighter here than anywhere in the states.

It was soon 11:00 pm and time for lights out, even though I heard talking long after that. I was happy to see everyone getting along. While attending Nyaka, these kids were put into competition with for grades and class position. A few held grudges. Those feelings seemed to evaporate during our evening of bonding.

The next morning, it was cold on the mountaintop. Our tents dripped with morning dew. Everyone, including me, wanted to stay within the warmth of their blanket, but I was not going to let them lay around for too long.

"Time to get up," I told the boys. "We have more hiking today."

Moans and groans sounded, but eventually the boys wandered to the fire pit area. They added sticks to create a small blaze.

I slapped the girls' tent. "It is morning. Time to rise and shine."

A few climbed through the doorway with blankets wrapped around their shoulders. I thought about winters in Michigan. How would they ever tolerate really cold weather?

The equatorial sun dried the tents quickly. The morning hike warmed everyone. We came to the end of my property. I reminded them that as awe-inspiring as the vista was, this mountain only overlooked one small valley. Still, I could not help but feel the immensity of the moment. This was the last stop before these students would fly off to begin their own life-journeys.

As a proud *taata*, I prayed for their success. Nothing was guaranteed. Even Hilary, whose walk had inspired Kutamba, had failed in the end. He was too old when he reached us, for his schooling to overcome the trajectory of his life. Most likely, he was tending goats on a Rukungiri District hillside as this group gazed down into the valley.

Tabitha took my hand. I leaned into her. I had always thought of myself as a man of two countries, but now I saw that was not true. I was...*we are* a family of the world. Tabitha, Nic, Nolan, Tessa and Talia. We will always be part of a greater whole.

Building Nyaka has given AIDs orphans a better life. It is a victory for them, for me, the entire community, but it is also much more.

AMANYA BONIETOR

Amanya Bonietor attended Kambuga Parents Primary School and St. Charles Lwanga Secondary School for O levels. Nyaka accepted her into the program and paid for her A levels at Immaculate Heart Girls School in Nyakibaale. She graduated from Makerere University with a Bachelors of Science in Nursing.

SARAH RIUNKADO

Sarah Riunkado attended Primary-Town Council Primary School in Rukungiri and Nyakabungo Girls Secondary School for O levels. The Nyaka program paid for her education at Bishop Comboni College in Kambuga and supported her until she received a degree in law from Uganda Christian University, Kampala Campus.

AFTERWORD

At the crack of a gun, 8:30 am on Sunday November 3rd, 2019, some 50,000 New York City runners will dash across the starting line to begin their grueling 26.4 mile marathon through five boroughs of the city, all hoping to reach the finish line in Central Park. Among the NYC multitude will be ten road-tested stalwarts who have raised money to educate Ugandan orphans, all wearing Nyaka T-shirts.

At the same hour of the morning (but eight hours earlier in Uganda), runners in Nyaka will begin their own marathon. Teachers, police officers, civil officials and other local residents will pursue a similarly daunting goal, but running 26.4 kilometers instead of miles, grateful for the support raised by their New York counterparts. In the lead will be Nyaka pioneer student, Aharizira Brendah, who ran marathons at university. Even Nyaka's grandmothers, who provide homes and second chances at life for thousands of extremely vulnerable children, will participate. In their "granny" uniforms, they will walk a full mile of the track in support of their kids.

Nowhere else on the planet will two such races—paired in purpose and spirit—happen on that same auspicious day. Who would have thought a chance meeting would have resulted in two incredible events?

It all happened on a December night in 2017, at the invitation of Mark and Noelle Mahoney, when I joined a small group for drinks and dinner at a hotel in mid-town New York. Jackson Twesigye Kaguri was in town! Mark, a new Nyaka board member, invited a few close friends to meet the founder of The Nyaka AIDS Orphans Project that we had heard so much about. Lucky me, to be included. In that one brief encounter—but with plenty of personal Q & A time—we heard unforgettable stories.

Jackson told us of his arrival in America, for example, on his way to his Columbia University fellowship. It was a bitterly cold January day when he arrived at JFK, after his first-ever plane ride, wearing light pants and a short-sleeve shirt. "But where's your coat?" his cab driver asked. "What's a coat?" Jackson answered. "But it's winter," the cabbie said. "What's winter?" Jackson asked. That response led to Jackson's first philanthropic gift in the U.S. His Senegalese cabbie drove him to a clothing store on Broadway where he bought Jackson (who had just one dollar in his pocket) a coat before depositing him on the Columbia campus for his graduate degree.

How fast Jackson's stories unfolded that evening! Like in 2001, when he went home to Nyaka on a visit and found it devastated by AIDS, his brother dying in his arms of the dreaded disease. His brother's last words were, "Take care of my children." How Jackson abandoned his American dream of owning a home in Indiana, and instead used his down-payment money to build (with his own hands and those of his friends) the first free two-room schoolhouse in his village. How that early effort remarkably escalated this year into educating some 950 kids, some all the way through university. And how 60,000 AIDS orphans now have homes in which to thrive.

I was awed and wasn't alone. Our entire group was dazzled by the enormity of his accomplishments. So, who wouldn't want to think of ways to support such a visionary—right? I thereupon posed a question: Was Nyaka registered for the NYC Marathon? "No,"Jackson said, "what's that?" I explained that some 400 non-profit organizations, vetted by Marathon officials, are given a certain number of "slots." Their racers, in exchange for the ability to run in the best-known and most competitive marathon in the world, individually raise funds for their particular charities. Intrigued, Jackson asked if Nyaka might get such a designation.

As a close friend of George Hirsch, founder and chairman of of the NYC Marathon, I happily took on the assignment. Trust me when I say Nyaka is an easy sell. After hearing the authentic story of how one man, born to uneducated parents in a poverty-stricken village, single-handedly changed the culture and hopes of thousands of people, any right-minded person would want to help. George was no exception. He quickly opened the race for Nyaka's application and provided six slots for the 2018 NYC Marathon.

The Mahoneys and I then set about planning an exciting weekend around the big race. "Coach Mahoney," as we dubbed him, took on the task of enlisting six enthusiastic runners who agreed to raise a minimum of $3000 each. According to Mark, it was a snap.

Runners for whom the NYC Marathon had been just a pipe dream quickly signed on. The first to step up was Julia Hoover, a young woman the Mahoneys had known since childhood, who offered to captain the team. Just as quickly, Julia's boyfriend, Donovan Walsh, signed on for his first marathon. As Julia previously had run several, he probably thought he'd better do some catching up. Next to volunteer was another young veteran, Arrington McCoy, who had run ten former marathons, but had never been able to crack the NYC line-up.

Mark then enlisted his friend Mark Semler, CEO of the Zucker Institute for Applied Neurosciences in Charlestown, who brought an innovative idea to the art of marathoning. Using the latest technology of Mark's Green Dot Bioplastics Company, he 3-D printed his running shoes from biomass material, thus demonstrating that his shoes could serve a valid purpose and then be composted instead of ending up in a landfill for thousands of years. And yes, the shoes made it, with Mark, all the way to the finish line.

Also joining the group were Ellen and Danny Harrison. Danny is the grandson of Barry Segal, founder of the Segal Family Foundation, which has been mentioned many times in this book as one of the most dedicated backers of Jackson's vision. Because his entrepreneurial wife, Ellen, runs her own events firm, she doubled as our catering planner for the Saturday luncheon.

Last of the lucky six was Sarah Ellsworth Garrett, new bride of my grandson, Taylor, so I had yet another reason to become intimately involved. This would be Sarah's first marathon, which added jitters to her months of training for the big event—and for good reason. Attempting to run a marathon is a strenuous, exhausting, and heartbreaking challenge if you fail, but an exuberant, thrilling, life-changing triumph if you finish. You've then proved to yourself—the only one who really matters—that you can set a goal and reach it, no matter how impossible it appears at the start.

All six of our runners set up rigorous training schedules as they began soliciting funds for Nyaka from family, friends, and colleagues in very personal terms on a website designed for that purpose.

Meanwhile, Noelle, Mark and I wanted the Marathon weekend to be a memorable experience not only for the runners, but for their families, friends, and donors as well. Mark approached a friend who owns a huge ping pong parlor and bar in midtown, who agreed to set aside party space for our crowd on Friday night where we could smack tiny white balls around while getting to know each other.

Coach Mahoney also organized a group of about 30 Nyaka supporters to jog the 5K warm-up run held by Marathon authorities on Saturday morning, starting in Dag Hammarskjold Plaza and ending at the Marathon's finish line. Mark and Jackson led this run to the delight (and laughter) of those who really know how to race. And to cap off the day before the Marathon, Noelle and I approached Uganda's Ambassador to the United Nations, Adonia Ayebare, who graciously offered to host a delightful luncheon for all our participants at his embassy.

Sunday was a brilliant blue-sky day—a relief after a cold, drenching rain the night before. At 6 am, Jackson and Coach Mahoney met our Nyaka Six at a designated subway stop that whipped them underground to the Staten Island Ferry, which sailed them over to the mammoth crowd of anxious runners on the Verrazano-Narrows Bridge. Starting time, 8:30 am. Our job as anxious families and friends, was to cheer our runners on while watching an app on our cell phones that showed exactly where each one was along the route. Cheer we did. We moved from the 57th Street Bridge, when they first came into Manhattan, to Lexington Avenue, then to the East Side of Central Park as they came down from Harlem, and finally to the finish line on the West Side. We yelled our hearts out, waving them on at each location.

Of course, we had no idea if any of our runners would actually finish the brutal course—nor did they. Taylor ran some 17 miles himself, checking on Sarah's progress. But to our surprise, the first to cross that magical goal line was our Sarah, radiant with triumphal joy, saying she loved every minute of her run. Then one by one, each of our Nyaka sorely-tested athletes crossed the finish to the applause and—let's be honest—relief of their nervous supporters. Wrapped in the blue Mylar capes given to all finishers, proud but exhausted, and on somewhat wobbly legs, they walked even more miles back to an East Side bar where they toasted each other's victory over the punishing course. Champions all!

To state that everyone was happy is an understatement. While the runners celebrated their personal triumphs, Nyaka banked $65,000 to educate more AIDS orphans and build more houses for their grannies. Jackson was so pleased that even before soreness left our runners' limbs, he began applying for ten slots for the 2019 NYC Marathon—and organizing his own marathon in Uganda. Typically thinking of his hometown, he wanted Nyaka folks to understand—and enjoy—the excitement and payoff that a marathon promises.

As I write this, Jackson is in fact so motivated that he has begun his own training schedule to join the Nyaka Ten in NYC on November 3rd. He has never run a race of any length. But he's a guy who, as a child, everyday ran seven miles to school, got a high school diploma in the top one percent of his class, earned a free college education, and received a graduate fellowship at Columbia University. So I wouldn't bet against him, would you?

Similarly, Jackson's immediate goal for 2020 is to raise the number of Nyaka's AIDS orphans living in loving homes to 100,000—a marathon in its own right. I wouldn't bet against him in that endeavor either, would you?

Sherrye Henry, New York City resident
and passionate volunteer for Nyaka

GLOSSARY

Agandi — How are you?

buzungu — humble name for a group of white persons

Baibuli Erikwera — Holy Bible

boda boda — Commercial motorbike used for public transportation like a taxi

buhorogye — Long time, no see.

embuzi — goat

enengo — rugged sharp ridge

ente — cow

gonja — roasted plantain

kabalagala — small sweet banana

maama — mother

matooke — steamed green bananas

muchomo — roasted chicken on a stick

mugaati — yeast bread

mukaaka — grandmother

Mureiregye — How did you sleep? (to a group)

muzungu — humble name for white person (plural is *buzungu*)

Nigye — I am fine

okutagurura — traditional dance

Oreiregye mzee — How did you sleep, old man?

posho — cornmeal

shwenkuru — grandfather

slim — slang for aids

taata — father

Webale — thank you

yego — Yes

ACKNOWLEDGMENTS

The Nyaka Program was born 18 years ago as of August 2, 2019. Many people have played a huge role since the program's inception.

To my wife Tabitha, and children Nicolas, Nolan, Talia, and Tessa. You inspire me every day. Tabitha, your EDJA Program that helps children survive sexual abuse has put 40 perpetrators in jail! This program compliments the holistic approach we hold dear in the Nyaka Program. You never cease to amaze me.

Nyaka pioneers who graduated university or are finishing medical or law school, I am proud of you and honored to be called "dad."

Special thank you to Catherine Inanir who advanced funds that made this book possible. Thanks to Lucy Y. Steinitz, Ph.D., Garret Turke, Ph.D, Paul Sutherland, Sherrye Henry, , Dr. Terri Kramer, Dr. Alison McNeal, Wendy Schneider, Richard G. Yates, and Brittany Linville Tonet for commenting on an early draft. Thanks to Brittany Linville Tonet and Matt Stauble for your photographs and dedicated spirits. Susan Linville, we have grown to be like brother and sister. Your hard work and dedication are unmatched.

Thank you to our Board and Advisors, past and present: Barbara Kroberger, Cath Inanir, Katherine Tillery, Dr. John Brewster, Mark Mahoney, J. Robin Langley, Tabitha Mpamira-Kaguri, Joy Adams, Dr. Lucy Steinitz, Dr. Amy Sarch, Dr. Andrew Pomerville, Jeffrey Boyce, Dr. Deborah Delmer, Diane Goldberg Hunckler, Marlene Laporte, Dr. Graham Pike, Mr. Seow Cheng Soon, Dr. Fred Tinning, Christopher Lowe, Dr. Sam Carpenter, Mr. Rolf Dietrich, Ms. Deborah Hutton, Dr. Jude Mugerwa, Ms. Carol Realini, Dr. Snea Thinsan, Dr. Dale Val, Carol Auld, Dr.

Richard Segal, Dr. Nancy Colier, Dr. Anu Frank-Lawale, Prof. Mondo Kagonyera, Justice Ogoola, Mr Larry Sallee, Ms. Jennifer Thomson, Mr. Aime Wata, Kevin Jaramillo, Kurt Gurter, Beronda Montgomery, Reneé Montgomery, and Shannon Johnson.

Thank you to our devoted staff. In the U.S.: Wendy Schneider, Daniele Reisbig, Dr. Sarah McCue, Cassandra Jones, Jane Kramer. In Uganda: Jennifer Natale, Shabnam Olinga, Sempa Abu Baker, Kaweesa Robert, Mugamba Jacqueline, Bymukama Hannington, Leah Kobusingye, Ivan Mwebesa, and Dr. Gayle Clilfford.

I would be remiss not to acknowledge our teachers, too numerous to list here. We would not survive without your dedication, hard work, and the nurturing you provide every day for our students.

Finally, to our volunteers, donors and supporters around the world: you have a special place in my heart. May you be blessed ten-fold with the love and hope we have received from you.

FOUNDATIONS

We are deeply appreciative of the foundations that have supported our efforts through the years. Their generosity, innovation and guidance has been invaluable.

Stephen Lewis Foundation, Segal Family Foundation, Nos Vies en Partage Foundation, Beautiful World, Women's Empowerment International, Epic Foundation, Global Giving, Rotary International, Korea International School, Imago Dei Fund, The Funding Network, Kiwanis International, CBD Charitable Trust, and 60 Million Girls

HELP MAKE A DIFFERENCE

1. Visit www.nyakaschool.org for information.
1. Become a friend of Nyaka and Twesigye Jackson Kaguri on Facebook and follow Jackson on twitter at twitter.com/twejaka
2. Recommend *A School for My Village* and *Victory for My Village* to friends, colleagues, book and women's clubs, religious groups, civic organizations, clubs, any group interested in education, literacy, cross-cultural issues, Uganda, HIV/AIDS prevention or alleviating poverty. Offer to lead a book discussion at your house of worship, library, or book club.
3. Propose *A School for My Village* and *Victory for My Village* for suggested reading at a school or university near you.
4. See if *A School for My Village* and *Victory for My Village* are in your local library. If not, donate a copy or suggest the book be added to their collection. Ask friends and family in other areas to do the same.
5. Encourage your local bookstore to carry the books if you don't see them on the store shelves.
6. Write a review of *Victory for My Village* for Amazon, Barnes & Noble, your local newspaper, radio station, or organization newsletter or create your own blog. Your comments help bring awareness to the book.
7. If you want to support our efforts directly, make a tax-deductible contribution to our nonprofit organization. Donate through our the Nyaka website. Donate once or become a Monthly Sustaining Donor. To give via check, please write to: **Nyaka AIDS Orphans Project PO Box 339 East Lansing, MI 48826**
8. Form a Friends of Nyaka Group or join one. Our friends groups help spread our message. Check our website to see

how to form your own group in your community or college campus.

9. Invite Twesigye Jackson Kaguri to speak at your conference, graduation, house of worship, library or civic organization—and bring lots of friends to hear him.

10. Become a Nyaka intern to serve others and change lives while gaining experience and building your resume. We offer limited internship opportunities in East Lansing and in rural Southwestern Uganda. Send an inquiry to internships@nyakaschool.org for information on internships in East Lansing or to info@nyakaschool.org for Uganda.

11. Become a Young Hero and use your creativity and talents to change lives. You can help children across the world today. Email us at info@nyaksachool.org for more information.

12. Is it your dream to run the TCS New York City Marathon? Why not run it for your students and grandmothers? You can learn more about the race on the TCS New York City Marathon website. As a team member, you will receive free entry to the NYC Marathon; free commemorative Nyaka race shirt; fundraising support and advice from the Nyaka team. All team members must commit to raise funds for Nyaka. We are looking for team members who can commit to raise at least $10,000.

13. Use our hashtag: #victory4myvillage

READING GROUP GUIDE

2. At the beginning of this book, a boy named Hilary walks 50 miles to find a school that he can attend for free. How does the public school system in Uganda differ from the school systems in other countries such as the United States and Europe? Did reading this book change your views about your own school system?

3. Many people in western Uganda are subsistence farmers who grow their own food or work on large farms called plantations. Most live in poverty. How does this affect their views on education? Do they treat education for girls and boys differently?

4. The Nyaka AIDS Orphans Project has donors large and small. Jackson considers all of them as essential. How do you judge the merits of an organization when considering a donation? Are some donations too small?

5. The Nyaka Project provides more than education to AIDS orphans. What other services does the organization provide? Is it necessary to deliver all the services? How are they interrelated?

6. The Nyaka Project helped two disabled students, Allan and Justine. How are disabilities viewed in the village? What options do they have to find medical care for people with disabilities? How does this compare to Special Needs and Disability options in your country or region?

7. Instead of being run by a foreign organization, the Nyaka project is headed by a Ugandan who knows the people, the region and the country. What are the advantages and disadvantages to this approach?

8. Jackson took several risks when it came funding his building projects. Do you think he took too many risks and was lucky when things worked out for the best? Do you think he should have taken fewer chances?

9. Organizations like the Stephen Lewis Foundation, Clinton Foundation, Global Citizen, and Segal Foundation are supporting organizations around the world. How have they helped the Nyaka Project?

10. The Nyaka Grandmother program now serves more than 10,000 grannies. What do you think of this approach of investing in women?

11. Some of the first students to attend Nyaka School have graduated from universities. What are your thoughts about the success of the Nyaka Project? Do you think having a secondary school as part of the program is beneficial?

12. After reading this book, have your views of Africa changed? Would you consider traveling to Uganda? Would you be interested in volunteering?

13. Did you read A School for My Village? Does your school, public library, or organization have a copy? If so, how was it obtained? If not, how can we get one to them?

FURTHER READING

If you found this book to be valuable, you will probably appreciate these books too.

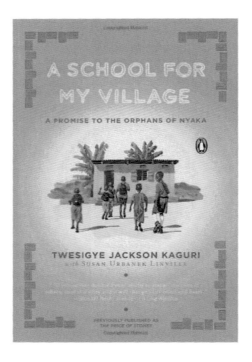

Can one person really make a difference in the world? Twesigye Jackson Kaguri overcame tremendous odds as he followed his dream to build a school for **AIDS** orphans in his village in Uganda. This is his unforgettable story.

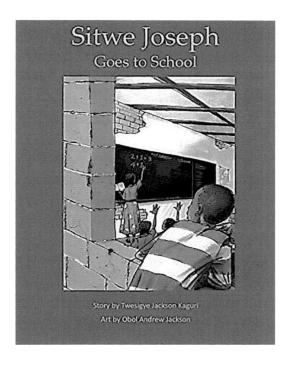

Story by Twesigye Jackson Kaguri

Art by Obol Andrew Jackson

Both of Sitwe Joseph's parents died from **HIV/AIDS**. Now he is an orphan living with his siblings and grandmother in a small village in Uganda, east Africa. Sitwe's sister takes life in stride, accepting all the hard work that is given to her. Sitwe is not ready to accept his lot. He dreams of going to school and is determined to find a way to get an education.

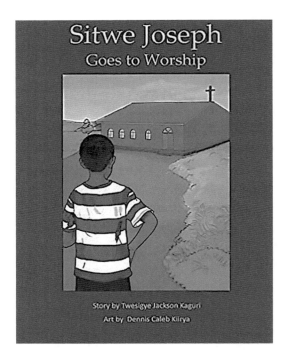

Sitwe Joseph
Goes to Worship

Story by Twesigye Jackson Kaguri
Art by Dennis Caleb Kiirya

Both of Sitwe Joseph's parents died from **HIV/AIDS**. Now he is an orphan living with his siblings and grandmother in a small village in Uganda, east Africa. When his little brother, Stephen, wanders from home and gets seriously hurt, Sitwe turns to prayer to help him.

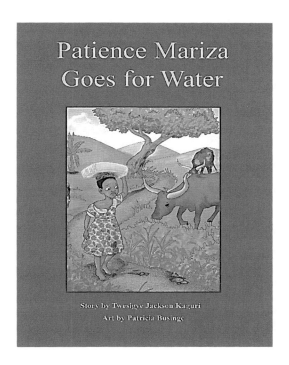

Patience Mariza
Goes for Water

Story by Twesigye Jackson Kaguri
Art by Patricia Businge

Both of Patience Mariza's parents died from **HIV/AIDS**. Now she
is an orphan living with an Uncle and Aunt in a small village in
Uganda, east Africa. Patience's aunt is cruel to her, but Patience
accepts all the hard work that is given to her until she encounters a
man at the river. Her life changes in many ways after this encounter.
She allows a neighbor woman to help her.

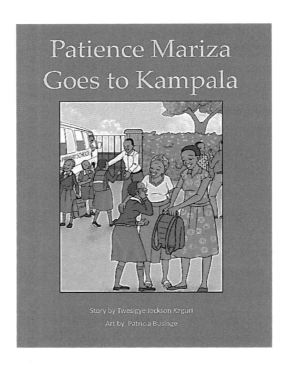

Patience Mariza
Goes to Kampala

Story by Twesigye Jackson Kaguri
Art by Patricia Businge

Patience Mariza lives in western Uganda where yearly exams must be taken for a student to pass on to the next years class. In this story, those receiving the highest test score will be offered an additional reward. They will get to travel to the capital city. Patience wants this more than anything and learns an important lesson not taught in books.